W0007770

V&R

Sylvia Schroll-Machl

Doing Business with Germans

Their Perception, Our Perception

With 3 Diagrams and 1 Table

5th Edition

Vandenhoeck & Ruprecht

The publication of this volume was supported by

Jörg Plannerer drew the 7 cartoons.

Bibliographic Information published by Die Deutsche Bibliothek

Die Deutsche Bibliothek lists this publication in the Deutsche
Nationalbibliografie; detailed bibliographic data are available
on the Internet at http://dnb.d-nb.de.

ISBN 978-3-525-46167-9
ISBN 978-3-647-46167-0 (E-Book)

Typeset by Satzspiegel, Nörten-Hardenberg
Printed and bound by ⊕ Hubert & Co, Göttingen
Printed in Germany

Contents

◼ Foreword

According to a 3000-year-old Chinese proverb concerning successful communication with strangers, "Only he who knows himself and his counterpart well can achieve one thousand successful encounters." Here the number one thousand really stands for an infinite number, thus guaranteeing success in all encounters for those who take heed of the proverb. In the context of international cooperation, a modern version of this ancient Chinese proverb could be: "Only those who really understand their foreign colleagues and themselves can achieve success in international business." The truth of this statement becomes obvious when we think about the vast amount of knowledge foreigners need to understand the style of working and living, the norms and standards, customs and traditions of the new country in which they are planning to live or work. When asked what motivated them to make their move, students planning to study at a foreign university, young people taking part in school and youth exchange programs, experienced managers and specialists taking part in international professional work exchange programs and many tourists planning a trip abroad often have the same spontaneous, simple answer: "I wanted to get to know the country and people better" or "I wanted to broaden my horizons." Many training and qualification programs – and even more travel and guide books – have attempted to meet the need for extensive and accurate information about foreign countries and their customs and traditions.

It is generally accepted that "global players" who are fit to "walk and work around the world" need to have a good measure of understanding, openness and curiosity about anything new and different, a dash of tolerance and, to round off the successful recipe, intercultural awareness.

Experienced travellers who have not been just visitors and spectators, but who have actually come to know a particular foreign country and have worked and forged common goals with their foreign partners, report that each new country represents a new and demanding challenge.

In the foreword of his book "Chinese Characteristics," published in Leipzig in 1900, Arthur H. Smith quotes Sir Robert Hard, General Director of the Chinese Customs Authority, who had lived and worked in China for over four decades: "China is a very difficult country to understand. A few years ago I believed that I had finally progressed so far that I was able to understand something of the country, and tried to write down my views. Today I feel like a complete novice again. If I were now required to write three or four pages about China, I would not know where to start. I have learnt only one thing. In my country we are told to stand firm and resist, even if this means that in the end we break. In China the opposite applies: let yourself be molded and changed, but don't allow yourself to break."

This statement is remarkable in many ways. First of all it shows that the more information and experience we gather about the people and culture of a foreign country, the greater our awareness of how little we actually know and understand of the supposedly "familiar" land and its inhabitants and how to get along with them. In addition Sir Robert Hard's comments make it clear that for him, his wealth of knowledge resulted not only from his many years of experience in dealing with and observing his Chinese partners, but was also in part due to his ability to reflect on his own country and culture.

Most people who, like Sir Robert Hard, report back on their experiences of a foreign country and its people, tend to speak exclusively about the things that have seemed strange, distinctive, incomprehensible or illogical. The foreign culture is the main focus. Our own culture functions as a yardstick against which to measure and judge the foreign culture, and is not often seen with fresh and critical eyes, as was the case for Sir Robert Hard. The second part of the Chinese proverb regarding "successful contact" refers to this self-knowledge, which is often lacking and therefore not taken into consideration.

International collaboration is often difficult for everyone involved because the behaviour of the respective foreign partners rarely matches their expectations of one another. To make the matter more complicated, the reasons for this unexpected behaviour are neither apparent nor comprehensible. This is, however, a very superficial and simplified view of the actual situation. The most serious challenge to international collaboration is not posed by lack of knowledge about each other, but lack of understanding of ourselves: of our own values, norms and rules, of how we perceive, think about and assess situations, of how we behave. We are completely unaware of how others perceive us and the effect we have on them. What is the reason for this lack of awareness of our own culture?

People from different nations and cultures who strive to work, communicate and cooperate together grew up in and were socialised within their own individual cultures. They were taught and came to accept the socially and culturally relevant norms, values and behaviours during this upbringing. As a result, they have adopted and individually adapted a very specific system of orientation which is typical for their culture. During the entire learning process the main characteristics of this culture-specific orientation system, which influences and governs thought, perception and behaviour, were taken for granted and accepted as a normal part of everyday behaviour, and therefore no longer noticed on a conscious level.

Everyday experience teaches us that other people can be expected to behave like us, and that our behaviour is generally accepted by others and is therefore *correct*. As a result we are convinced that people acting with good intentions will (or should) act as we have learnt to, and as we have experienced as positive and successful: our assumptions have never been challenged. If we meet someone whose behaviour does not meet our expectations, we automatically interpret this behaviour negatively, as being the product of ignorance, incompetence or unwillingness – or we may even suspect some ulterior motive.

Of course we know that people from other nations and cultures behave differently to a certain extent, along the lines of "other countries, other customs," and we are therefore ready and willing to accept a certain level of difference. If, however, this behaviour deviates too far from our expectations or, even worse, contradicts one of our own important behavioural norms, we can no longer be tolerant. Behaviour that once intrigued us as being "exotic" can instantly become *something that needs to change* and deserving of training, reprimanding, correction or perhaps even some other more radical form of indoctrination. Even when the whole basis for cooperation between international partners is in dire danger because of varying expectations and behavioural differences, it is rare that either side will stop and reflect upon how their own culturally-created behaviour has contributed to the problem.

The way we perceive and interpret a situation occurring in an international setting depends on our own cultural orientation system, which in turn reflects only one possible approach among many. It is only natural that the actions of a foreign partner will seem strange, and for this reason it is important that each person in an international setting recognises the situation in its entire complexity, and defines it as *inter*cultural; as *different* and not strange and wrong. Intercultural experiences, no matter how dramatic and extreme, unfortunately do not automatically trigger a process that helps us to understand our own cultural orientation better. Instead, this level of awareness can only be achieved when very specific cultural information is available, as well as the means to apply it.

This book was written for exactly this purpose: to provide the information and examples necessary for recognising and understanding the intricacies of German culture. Anyone who has grown up with German culture, and who needs or wants to deal successfully with people from different cultures, will gain insight into their own culture and their own cultural orientation, which in turn will enable them to better understand their experiences with foreigners. Germans will learn to understand how their behaviour looks from the outside and, in this way, can learn how to modify their behaviour in intercultural settings to make the cooperation more productive, enjoyable and successful.

The experience on which this book is based does not come from philosophical, historical or psychological research by Germans about Germans. Instead, it comes from the sharing of many first-hand observations and experiences of Germans by foreigners. This book concentrates on their observations of the culturally specific German behaviours which have perplexed them and caused them considerable problems and grief. Their observations and insights are surprisingly similar despite their differing nationalities.

What German readers of this book can learn is the result of systematic collection and analysis of those behaviours which foreigners have repeatedly identified as "typically German." We can only begin to understand our own culturally specific orientation system and the effect it has on our foreign partners when we begin to look at ourselves from *their* perspective.

For the non-German reader, this book represents an excellent source of information on the culturally specific orientation system that makes something "typically German." Some of the most strongly rooted typical German culture standards include:

Objectivism (objectivity, task-focus); appreciation for rules, regulations and structures; rule-oriented, internalised control; time planning; separation of personality and living spheres; low-context communication and, finally, individualism.

This book attempts to define culture, culture standards, the limitations and possibilities presented by these definitions, and the part played by history in their development in the German context. The main part of this book deals with the detailed description of the central German culture standards and an exact analysis of how they form the basis of German behaviour. It also analyses the advantages and disadvantages of each culture standard with regard to interpersonal communication and cooperation. Suggestions are offered on how to resolve the resulting challenges and problems. Recommendations on dealing with the culture standards are made for both non-Germans working with Germans and Germans working internationally.

This book is distinctive because it is based on real-life experiences and was designed to be used in real-life situations. These real-life experiences are not a collection of random, unrelated events put together without rhyme or reason by the author. Instead, they are firmly anchored in a scientifically researched concept of culture, in which culture is seen as an orientation system, which in turn is determined and defined by specific culture standards. Furthermore, it gives German readers the necessary tools to master the difficult task of perceiving and understanding their own system of orientation within German culture, which is the prerequisite for understanding and dealing with the behaviour of their foreign partners. For non-German readers, this book provides a wealth of information to aid their understanding of the peculiarities of German behaviour which have previously been incomprehensible, and have had a negative effect on their interactions with Germans. In this way, everyone will be better equipped to deal effectively, productively and enjoyably with each other.

This book provides excellent educational material for learning how to approach intercultural encounters and exchanges so as to get the most out of them. Each partner, German and non-German, will be able to harness the culture-specific resources involved in their intercultural encounters as effectively as possible. The material can either be used as a self-study-guide or to accompany intercultural coaching and vocational training programmes.

This book will help you to achieve one of the most important factors for future international success: intercultural competence.

Alexander Thomas

■ Introduction

■ Why a Book about Germans?

With globalisation becoming ever more pervasive in everyday life, many people are faced with challenging new situations. Cultural differences no longer fascinate only tourists and intrigue academics, they present very real and everyday challenges to people working internationally:

- expatriates, who live abroad with their families for a period of time;
- people working for a company in their own country, but who end up on foreign business trips as much as at home because of an increasingly international customer base;
- members of an international team, or of a "virtual team" scattered around the globe;
- companies with subsidiaries abroad, where colleagues in the various locations work in close contact with one another;
- companies experiencing post-merger integration difficulties where employees now have to cooperate with new colleagues in different countries;
- companies which have been acquired or sold where the employees now have to adjust to a foreign management style;
- in search of an appropriate job, some people may only find adequate and attractive positions abroad (brain-drain emigrants);
- and the list goes on!

Whether they like it or not, all of the people in these situations are faced with the challenge of having to communicate and interact with people from countries other than their own. This book is about dealing with this challenge, with a very specific context in mind: amongst the industrial nations, Germany is an important player in international business. For this reason many non-Germans have to get along with Germans, be it as guests in Germany or in their own countries. Likewise, many Germans come into daily contact with people of all nationalities on a business level, be it face to face or via modern tele-communications. For non-Germans, it is important to have as much information about Germans as possible in order to be prepared. It is also very interesting for Germans to learn how their non-German partners view them and to see themselves from a different perspective. Only by keeping the other person's perspective in mind can they adjust to the specific behaviour and expectations of their counter-parts, monitor their own culturally determined behavior and be less decidedly German, depending upon what the situation calls for.

This is why I called this book: "Doing Business with Germans: Their Perception, Our Perception." It is important for me to begin from the foreigners' viewpoint of Germans, so that Germans can learn to understand how they are seen from the outside. It is also vital that non-Germans can reflect upon their observations and experi-ences with understanding of the German perspective, so that they can come to understand what Germans really mean when they say or do something.

Both perspectives are especially important when we begin to dis-cuss *intercultural competence* and what it means: understanding of the *cultural logic* of others (for the non-Germans) and insight into one's own culture (for the Germans). Hopefully, this book will help both sides to achieve this.

■ What this Book Holds for You

I am both an experienced intercultural trainer and have completed research at the University of Regensburg in intercultural psychology. I want to share with you the knowledge I have been able to accumu-late during the many intercultural training sessions I have held as well as the results of my research at the Regensburg Institute of Psy-chological Research. The stories and examples in this book either re-late to professional work experiences in Germany or with German companies or stem from the everyday experiences of expatriates liv-ing in Germany. These stories and examples have been recounted, acted out or observed during my seminars, coaching sessions and research interviews. They offer a clear picture of how non-Germans view Germans and their behaviour, and what they classify as "typical" for Germans.

Behaviour follows certain rules, and I will be talking about the motivation behind the way Germans behave. My goal is to help the reader to understand this motivation and therefore the behaviour it gives rise to. Reflection on one's own culture is always difficult but necessary in order to explain the logic behind it to foreigners who want to understand us better. I have also attempted to explain the historical background which formed the German character and to make it more understandable.

■ Which Germans are Described in this Book?

When I speak to a German audience and refer to the "German character" I inevitably get the response: "I'm sorry, but I have to disagree. I come from Bavaria/Cologne/Hamburg (or some other place) and what you say is only partially true there. You really have to distinguish between the Northern Germans/Bavarians/Swabians (or some other German regional grouping)." Or they say something like, "Yes, that's how it used to be, but now the situation is different ..." (meaning, of course, that it has improved). These reactions exemplify the first, and in my opinion one of the most deeply rooted, German characteristics: No-one wants to be deemed typical. It is always the others who are "typical Germans" – persons from other regions, from other social groups, or only the men or the older generation – "But I'm not that way at all – not completely – anyhow." From an historical point of view this is all quite understandable, since Germany has only existed as a united nation since 1871 (or since 1990 depending upon how you view it), and for this reason there is no long tradition of a common German identity.

Nevertheless, let me say the following – especially to my non-German readers:
1. Your own cultural background is the major deciding factor which determines how you understand what I will describe. Many of the cultural traits may seem familiar to you; the differences may be very difficult for you to understand; and in some cases a trait may

be stronger in your own culture than in Germany. This is because there are areas of similarity between cultures, and it could be that your culture is very close to that of Germany in some or many aspects, but in others very different. Since this book is about the most obvious differences which many people from a wide variety of countries notice about German culture, and deals with generalisations helpful to an outsider looking in, there will be times when you see little difference and others where you see a lot. I can only ask for your patience and understanding – keep on reading until what I have to say is more relevant to you and your culture.

2. It is not my goal to say anything negative that could create a gulf between Germans and non-Germans. Instead I wish to share the experiences that foreign colleagues have shared with me, sometimes expressing humour and surprise, other times disappointment and offence. My wish is to make German culture more understandable and so to improve the quality of our interactions. Unfortunately, negative experiences such as disappointment, frustration and anger are often the first ones registered, and they lead to the wrong conclusions and make it difficult to break through barriers. If we can learn intercultural competence, we can avoid much frustration and end up with a much more pleasant working relationship between non-Germans and Germans.

3. What I have to share with you in this book is what Germans regard as normal, everyday behaviour: things which are considered correct, appropriate and usual. I have attempted to explain the ideological background to "typical German behaviour" so as to help non-Germans deal with it without irritation and anger. As a non-German, you need to understand these things and know what to expect so that you can be prepared. Once you know a bit about what to expect, adjusting to living in Germany or working with and getting along with Germans becomes a lot easier. It is not my intention, however, to defend or apologize for what would be considered rudeness and bad behaviour even by Germans. Unfortunately, such examples do occur. Once you have read this book and have an overview of German culture standards, you will be better able to distinguish between what is typically German (even when it may be rude in your culture) and why, and what is just bad manners independent of cultural differences. You will then be able to distinguish between experiences which can be generalised and

those which are one-off, and avoid putting them together. This will help you stay happy and motivated in your interactions.

To my German readers, I would like to say:

1. As soon as we speak of the German character, most Germans automatically expect the worst and automatically want to exclude themselves from any such generalisation. This situation repeats itself over and over again. As soon as we make *any* attempt to make a list of typical German characteristics with a group of foreigners, it is seen by Germans as a bad omen. Strangely enough, however, the word "likeable" never appears on this list, although "friendly" appears more often. Germans try to defend themselves by saying, "Yes, but there's a positive side to being this way. In this way we can always be sure that everything is being managed effectively and efficiently." At least this is how they explain themselves about 90% of the time. Only rarely can Germans accept a description of their "typically German characteristics" from a neutral standpoint. My German readers may also find it hard to be neutral. It is worthwhile to keep the following in mind. What I have to say about Germans is not all bad, and I certainly am not criticising anyone. The traits and characteristics I call "typically German" have just as many pros and cons as those of people from any other country.

2. Of course, Germans are right to be sceptical! A pharmacologist who understood my dilemma once explained it to me as follows. He said that any study having to do with "living biological matter" can only be discussed in terms of probabilities – there can be no absolutes, because there are always exceptions. A statement about a generalisable empirical result, which is true for many cases, has already taken normal deviation into consideration and, to be accepted as correct, describes *tendencies*. Judge for yourself: as you read each chapter, you are sure to recognise many different Germans with whom you may have come into contact. And certainly you will say to yourself repeatedly: "But my friends and colleagues aren't that way." Any German who is honest with themselves will sometimes recognise themselves in these examples, other times not at all. Behaviour is determined by a myriad of factors, not just cultural influences, and it is these factors together with the situation which determine how we behave. Additionally, each person will respond differently to a set of circumstances depending on

their personality, and on the choices they make: we all have "room to move" and can make conscious decisions about how we behave. Nevertheless, the simplified and generalised observations and statements in this book correspond to the collective "truth" of real life.

3. German readers should keep in mind that regional and gender-specific differences that they see are only minimally noticed by foreigners and are not relevant to a portrayal of "the bigger picture." Such fine differences will only be perceptible to a foreigner who has lived in Germany for a very long time. This is also true for the influence of recent history on the development of German characteristics. Germans tend to emphasise the developments and changes that have occurred in their personal values and behaviour from the standpoint of what those values and behaviours used to be. Foreigners cannot do this: they only see Germans as they are now, using their own cultural orientation as a yardstick. Accordingly, whereas Germans may see themselves as having become softer and more relaxed with regards to rules and regulations which were previously written in stone, outsiders will still see them as comparatively obsessed with such structures and allowing their lives to be more strictly ruled than is normal in many other cultures.

The people who are described in this book and who provided the examples come from many different countries. Most are from countries where my employers have business contacts: Western, Central and Eastern Europe, the United States, Brazil, Australia, India, Japan and China. People from other cultures and countries will certainly have had similar experiences, but they have not been in any of my seminars. At the start of each chapter in the section called "How Germans are Perceived by Other Cultures" you can read a range of spontaneous responses from foreigners who were asked about characteristics they had particularly noticed. These responses are neither representative of the broad population nor complete, and agreement or disagreement with them will vary from person to person, or culture to culture.

Nevertheless, it is true that, regardless of their own cultural orientation, the observations made by non-Germans are very similar. By putting together the many-faceted reports, which look at Germans from many different angles, we can put together a picture of "typical" German behaviour. Germans cannot ignore this feedback;

given the importance of careers and professionalism to them, they cannot afford to disregard the impression they make on their foreign colleagues. These impressions cannot be viewed as strange quirks but must be understood. After all, we are talking about work, not play.

Although it would be easier to refrain from "stereotyping" what is "typically" German, especially since the negative aspects come quicker to the fore, this would mean sacrificing a useful tool for intercultural understanding and orientation. Paradoxically, the more complicated the situation, the more useful the stereotypes become.

■ Acknowledgments

In recognition that this book is not the product of one single person, I wish to thank the many people who helped to make it possible. During my intercultural training sessions on Germany I was very fortunate to be able to experience the vast breadth of reactions to the theme "The Germans." The participants were able to tell their stories and express their opinions, sometimes in the form of role-plays which obviously had a cathartic effect on them. I observed questioning faces, heard about trials, annoyances and disappointments, and all related to the theme "The Germans." After the dust from these eruptions had settled, it was my job to try to explain what had happened from the German perspective, and to try to give plausible explanations of what lay behind the German behaviour in question: why they did and said something. I was often able to help my foreign audience to understand the situations better, the "aha!" effect of the penny dropping and things making sense, which is a positive result producing a more positive view of the Germans. The Germans who took part in these discussions were extremely interested and found them very illuminating about their own behaviour; so much so that I was encouraged to write about and share this knowledge and these experiences. I wish to express my thanks to all of the participants of my seminars who shared with me so openly. I wish to thank the personnel managers who decided to hold these training sessions and to continue them on a regular basis. I also want to express my gratitude and thanks to everyone who was so supportive during the writing of this book, especially Andrina Rout for lending her language skills. With respect to the scientific side of this book, I also wish to thank all those who participated in my many research interviews for giving their time and commitment, especially Professor Thomas and all of the colleagues in his department, for their willingness to share their entire collection of information with me.

What are Culture Standards?

The Basis

When two people from different cultures have to deal with one another, each person initially behaves "completely normally," meaning in the way a typical Chinese, Brazilian, American, Russian or German would behave in a particular situation. Because both of them have to interact in order to achieve their goals, problems occur when what is deemed "normal behaviour" in China, Brazil, America or Russia deviates from how the other person would behave in the same situation. Both people feel alienated and irritated because their modes of action are not compatible with one another.

If people from different cultures have little or no knowledge about the cultural norms and characteristics of each other, they have no choice but to act in accordance with the social patterns and rules they have learned in their own culture, and to evaluate the interaction in terms of what their definition of "normality" is. Consequently, they often fail to consider that different ways of dealing with every day life or work situations might exist; instead, they deem their own, well-known ways to be the only sensible ones available.

Should these people continue to work together, the situation often becomes increasingly difficult and conflict-ridden, making it very stressful for everyone. Each one attempts to adjust, control and make sense of their own behaviour as well as that of the other using their own cultural orientation. However, the cultural orientation system that individuals acquired during their own socialisation will fail in this situation, because it is not able to understand and anticipate the behaviour of someone from another culture. For this reason people often act and react inappropriately: they misunderstand one another, misread situations, feel insecure and, in extreme cases, are completely incapable of taking action.

The whole process is a complex one:

1. First, we try to explain and understand the different and disturbing behavior of the other person. To do so, we usually resort to imagining how we would interpret a similar situation in our own culture. We also take into account all the information available about the other person's culture, and this knowledge may largely consist of prejudices and stereotypes.

2. Then the correction process begins. We want to correct the unexpected effect our behaviour has had on the other person. Both people now concentrate on the problems in communication and begin a number of more or less accurate reflective and analytical processes. At worst, the tried and tested strategies from our own culture are implemented and the gap widens. At best, other methods of regulating the interaction are tried, which at least partly take the views and behavioural patterns of the other person into consideration. This may lead to a de-escalation of the situation.

This procedure is strenuous because it is laden with obstacles. Because there is so much information on which to reflect and sort out, considerable time and energy is needed to correct and adjust our way of thinking and acting. Since the effects of any interactive action taken are uncertain, every situation becomes heavily laden with stress and tension and "Business as usual" becomes impossible.

The solution to this dilemma is to acquire more information about the other culture, so that (1) the explanations become more accurate and (2) we can choose the best corrective strategy. Our own cultural orientation system has to be expanded to incorporate understanding of the foreign culture. Both orientation systems must be used. This is why I am trying to impart to my non-German readers a glimpse of the "German soul." On the other hand, Germans need to be aware of their own cultural and behavioural patterns. Only then can they can identify the sensitivities of others and restrain from doing things which approach the "pain threshold." These are my reasons for delving into and analysing the German way of thinking and behaving in such detail.

Unfortunately, problems in intercultural interactions can cause considerable damage to international business relations, creating time-consuming setbacks and unpleasant disturbances. The worst problem is that initially, the problems and the perils may be well hidden or underestimated. After all, we are all just human beings. We all see, hear, love, hate and fight; we all want to work and to achieve something; we all want the best for our families. We may be speaking different languages, but surely this is a surmountable problem. But the fact is that we all see, hear, love, hate, fight, work and care for our loved ones quite differently. Our goals in life may nominally be the same, but the methods we use to reach them are quite different, and this is exactly the point at which our difficulties begin. First and foremost, these problems are rooted in invisible cultural differences (convictions, opinions, values and attitudes), all of which demand and deserve a great deal of respect. If the people interacting could only respect *each other's* values, then the relationships would succeed.

◼ The Definition of Culture

To what extent is it possible in this context to speak of cultural differences? I admit that the question may sound pompous, but it is technically valid to pose it, as definitions of culture are convoluted and extremely variable. I too use the term in a specific way and have adopted the following definition, which is in accordance with Kroeber und Kluckhohn's (1952) analysis of varying culture definitions and is also based on the theoretical works of Boesch (1980):

– Culture imparts meaning. Through culture, objects and events take on an order, a sense, a function and a meaning and become tangible to individuals, groups, organisations and nations.
– Culture offers mankind a way of thinking about and dealing with physical and theoretical matter. Our own culture also sets boundaries around how things should be dealt with.
– Throughout human history, each group of people has come up with a different system of defining and orientating themselves using their own concepts regarding sense, meaning and purpose. Cultures are the result of this process.
– Cultures have always existed, and during the course of time every culture has been transformed by internal and external influences.
– Culture serves as an orienting force in a world where the rise and fall of events can be overwhelming.

Cultural orientation is never static; rather it develops in response to the need to fulfill the basic requirements of life in a particular time and place. These requirements in turn are partly the result of the effects of living conditions over time. Cultures have an historical perspective.

In this way, culture can be considered "a universal orientation system typical for a society, organisation or group. This orientation system is created from specific symbols relevant to the society or group in question and are handed down from generation to generation. It influences the way in which its members perceive, think, value and act, and thus defines their membership within the society. Culture as an orientation system lays out and offers a mode of behaviour for the individuals who feel that they belong to this society, and on this basis creates the prerequisites necessary to develop a distinctly perceptible form of dealing with one's environment" (Thomas 1996a, p. 112).

■ The Definition of Culture Standards

The main themes of this book are based on the view that culture is a specific orientation system, comprising individual cultural elements which are related to each other in a systematic, structured way. These elements have resulted from the interaction of individuals with each other and with their environment. They have been passed on in more or less the same form over the generations and have a clear influence on all areas of life. These cultural elements have the effect of simplifying complexities and of offering behavioural guidance. They make the actions and behaviour of individuals within the cultural framework predictable and thus provide a basis from which expectations can be formed. These cultural elements are termed "culture standards" and can be defined as follows:

"Culture standards can be seen as the socially shared and accepted norms and values that are used by the individuals living within a particular culture to evaluate the behaviour of each other. Culture standards are used to set standards, limits and to establish a frame of reference against which to measure behaviour. They are the central characteristics that define a culture. They serve as the orientation system for perception, thought and behaviour. They provide the members of a culture with a yardstick against which they can measure their own and others' behaviour, so as to decide what is normal, typical and acceptable, and what is not. Culture standards function as implicit theories or rules and are internalised by the individual during the process of socialisation. Culture standards consist of a central *norm* and a *realm of tolerance*. The norm provides the ideal. Deviations from the norm will exist and those that are still acceptable, will lie within the realm of tolerance." (Thomas 1999, pp. 114 f.).

The following points are of primary importance:

- When Germans and non-Germans come in contact with one another, they will mainly notice behaviour which contradicts what they expect. This may be interesting, or it may be irritating, annoying or an obstruction. Other behaviour will go largely unnoticed. This is because our own cultural orientation system controls and directs our *perceptions.*
- The cultural orientation system regulates our values: people who have to deal with others in business situations are usually in this type of role because their own culture has deemed them to be suitable. They are viewed within their culture as skilled professionals, judged on the basis of their past performance and successes as being ideally suited to international exchanges. Thus, both the Germans and the non-Germans are naturally convinced that their way of doing things is the right and most effective way, and they feel completely justified in accusing the other person of being difficult and counter-productive. "Any other method is too strange, too peculiar, and most definitely impossible! You simply can't do it that way! That is just not going to work! Our way makes sense, it is the best way and it is the right way." Culture standards offer us a form of orientation to guide us through the process of deciding which mode of behaviour is normal, typical, and acceptable and conversely, which mode of behaviour is unacceptable.
- Culture standards define characteristics on an abstract and generalised level. They relate to those elements an entire nation has in common. They do not, however, attempt to define individuals, and a real-life German, such as your boss or colleague can and will deviate quite considerably from these standards! It is even possible that only a fraction of the standards described will apply to one particular individual. There may be culture standards which cannot be attributed to an individual at all, or which fit the next person perfectly.

Deviations from the culture standards exist and are accepted; in other words, there is a realm of tolerance. Variations from the culture standards of specific individuals and groups are accepted *as long as they lie within* the realm of tolerances: if not, they are rejected. This situation can be seen in the following diagram:

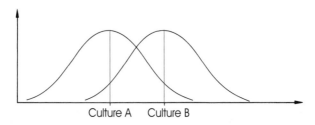

Culture A   Culture B

Diagram 1: Normal distribution

A culture standard does not have the same strength in each member of a society or culture. A central norm corresponds to the expectation value of what is being measured and the actual range of variation to the statistically calculated standard deviation. This means that when we compare two cultures, members of one culture will demonstrate a more extreme level of a particular mode of behaviour than found in the other culture: the characteristics observed have different levels of prominence. Thus, with the help of culture standards I am able to describe certain behaviours as being typical for "the average German." The variations in typical behavior can be measured quantitatively. However, because we initially notice the *differences* between ourselves and others, cultural differences as a whole may often seem greater and more unbridgeable than they in fact really are. We tend to focus our perception on the areas in which we are *different* without noticing all those we have in *common*, and we also tend to blow these differences out of proportion.

– From this dichotomy of interests – adapting to society on the one hand and maintaining individuality on the other – the dynamics of a culture arise. A certain amount of flexibility is necessary within each norm of behavior. If a norm is too strict, the society loses its capability to adapt and develop. Cultures are not static, but constantly undergoing change. This process of change, though it occurs relatively slowly, becomes apparent when innovations are introduced by minority groups and are only much later accepted by the majority. Every culture has to adapt to new demands. Discrepancies in behaviour are even expected of certain individuals and groups. They are needed to give impetus to the change process. No matter how many variations there are of the culture standards within a culture, when compared to the culture standards of another society, the deviations of a minority group are not the first thing that meets the eye. What is more readily noticed is the behaviour of the majority. However, because of the dynamics of cultural standards, deviations from the norm exist and I will strive to describe them for you whenever possible. I will also try to explain the historical development of each culture standard.

– Generally speaking all non-Germans and their behaviour are judged by Germans on the basis of the existing German culture standards. The more that behaviour corresponds to the standards, the better the individual is accepted. Non-Germans are often judged more harshly than other Germans. This may be seen in the fact that they are allowed a far smaller range of deviation on any given standard than their German counterparts. The observance of these cultural rules or standards is, as it were, the entrance examination for foreigners wishing to be accepted into society. Any non-German can confirm this.

■ Limitations to the Concept of Culture Standards

The concept of culture standard I support is not undisputed. It is the subject of major criticism, with which I partially agree. The main problem is the fact that it greatly reduces the complexity of reality. The concept of culture standards may even be guilty of promoting stereotyping. I cannot stress enough that the generalisations made here about "the Germans" are based on the prevailing tendencies within a national group, and are not meant to be representative of the behaviour and mentality of *all* its members. In real life you never meet up with "the German," but rather you will be confronted with a genuine individual from the whole population of Germans. This means you will meet Germans who are nice, likeable, well-mannered, open-minded, humorous, and competent in their job: or perhaps they will be completely unlikeable, grim, ill-tempered and incompetent.

Changes in mood and feelings also blur the inherent character traits of an individual. There simply does not exist an individual whose thinking, feelings and actions always correspond exactly to the culture standards of their respective culture. Cultural identity has a decisive influence on the identity of an individual, but it is also heavily influenced and complemented by the individual personality. It is precisely this interplay that defines the spectrum of available adaptation processes and possibilities for change within a culture. This is the prerequisite for successful collaboration between individuals, despite whatever cultural differences there may be.

Situations and structures also produce variables which in turn influence behaviour:
- the conditions of the contact (duration, intensity, willingness),
- the affiliation to minority groups within the respective culture (occupational groups, corporate field, organisational culture, educational status, social status),
- how those involved envisage their goals and their level of compatibility to one another,
- the balance of power and power structures,
- the status of the groups and individuals involved,
- the field of business in which the people are involved,
- any possible competition taking place between them,
- all current and concrete goals and interests,
- the dominant social climate of wherever the meeting is taking place (a company's corporate culture).

As the author, I am fully aware that reality is much more complex and multi-layered, and that this complexity must always be kept in mind when reading the generalisations and standardisations used in this book to describe culture standards.

The use of culture standards is just one way of preparing, planning and analysing certain situations in which the cultural factors that contribute to good working conditions between Germans and non-Germans can be recognised and labelled. All individuals involved as well as the respective situations are also major contributing factors to the success! People are more used to taking the individual factors and the situational elements into consideration than they are

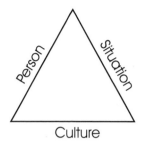

Diagram 2: Triangle ("Person-Situation-Culture")

to considering the various cultural factors. Therefore, this book claims that it is legitimate to spend time describing the cultural level so that it too can be used as an international management tool. Put simply: cultural standards can be used to explain and clarify about a third of all issues revolving around non-German and German relations. Unfortunately no more, but also no less.

■ How are Culture Standards Generated?

In order to define culture standards, intercultural psychologists employ the method of collecting and analysing so called *critical incidents* (Thomas 1988). When difficult and problematic "critical" situations occur, the "adjusting" effect of culture standards on the behaviour of the participants becomes evident, as each person behaves according to the standards they acquired during their respective socialisation. Because every culture takes their culture standards for granted, it is necessary to take a close look at them in order to firstly, become aware of them and secondly, to understand them as something defined by human beings and not a given. This requires both cultures to confront each other on the points which are taken for granted by their own culture but which differ from those of the other culture.

In order to *really* be able to see the differences in cultural orientation, it is important to find areas of contrast. This occurs in the everyday work world, in which Germans and non-Germans have to work together, especially at the points where the cultural orientation systems differ strongly from one another. Those patterns of behaviour which are unexpected, incomprehensible, irritating or even alarming from the perspective of the members of the other culture need to be examined methodically. Why?

The reason is that we use culture standards to guide us in making our behavioural choices; as a way of reaching our interactive goals. Both the goal and the way we achieve it is important.

"Only where there is cultural behaviour which is contrary to what would be expected can the contrast between the two cultures be perceived. Extreme deviations from behavioural expectations make it easier for scientists to take a look at the underlying system of cultural orientation than if they were looking at normal situations and processes" (Molz 1994, S. 80).

Such critical incidents are reported in research interviews and are recounted and played out in intercultural training sessions. The participants describe incidents in which the behaviour of Germans has been particularly noteworthy. In other words, any experiences or observations that have been odd or disturbing and that they have not been able to understand. Why do German behave in this or that way? These "critical experiences" are then explained by Germans. Offering the German point of view has the advantage that all non-Germans can get good, solid answers to their questions. Germans, on the other hand can benefit from this process of analysis as well, especially if they use it as an opportunity to take a good look at their own behaviour and thoughts.

Why are Germans the way they are? What do they actually mean when they say one thing or another? What are their "true" intentions when they behave in a certain way? What are the reasons (causal attribution), what are the goals (final attribution), and what are some other possible explanations for their behaviour? Culture standards represent the summation and abstraction of all of the explanations that have been collected from a large number of critical incidents. They differ clearly from stereotypes and prejudices. Culture standards are not the result of the various opinions and attitudes that non-Germans have about Germans, but rather they are based on *actual situations* that foreigners have experienced and which have been analysed and explained by *Germans*.

■ Central German Culture Standards

Recent research has furnished us with an abundance of German culture standards which are useful and usable when looking at critical incidents. In Table 1 are the results of a study in which Americans and Germans (Markowski et al. 1995), French and Germans (Molz 1994), Czechs and Germans (Schroll-Machl 2001) and Chinese and Germans (Thomas et al. 1996) are contrasted with one another.

Table 1: German cultural standards in comparison to other nations.

In contrast to USA	In contrast to France	In contrast to Czech Republic	In contrast to China
personal property	objectivism	objectivity/task-orientation	objectivism
rule orientation need for organisation	rule and stability orientation	appreciation of structures	rule orientation
	systematic job completion	consecutiveness	time planning
conscientious	self motivation, independence of working	rule orientation control	contract bound
boundaried private sphere interpersonal distance differentiation gender differentiation	separation of spheres of life	separation of personality and living spheres	separation of work and private spheres
direct interpersonal communication	explicit, direct communication	low context conflict confrontation	directness/truthfulness/honesty
	public spirit		individualism
respect for authority	quest for equality		
		stable self assurance	
physical proximity			

Here one can see that there are a number of German culture standards which are viewed as important, even from different cultural viewpoints. The following culture standards are presented in this book and illustrated with numerous examples:

- *Objectivism: objectivity and task focus*
- *Appreciation for Rules, Regulations and Structures*
- *Rule-Oriented, Internalised Control*
- *Time Planning*
- *Separation of Personality and Living Spheres*
- *"Low context": the German Style of Communication*

Particularly for readers from outside the Western world (for example, Southern Asia, Eastern Asia and Russia), I feel it is important to describe a further "Western" culture standard called *"Individualism,"* which I will describe as it is found amongst Germans.

■ Putting it all into Perspective

Before I present the results of my intercultural training sessions and research, I would like to put the following points into perspective:

1. I do not claim to fully characterise German culture, nor do I intend to dictate how the "typical German" always reacts in a professional context. I have chosen to concentrate on the essentials, which have caused the most amazement and discussion in almost all of the intercultural training sessions I have conducted. Only the emphasis differs slightly depending upon the cultural origin and individual background of the participants. Of course, there are many other aspects that could be mentioned, but it would be impossible to cover all of these in one book.

2. For this reason I have chosen to concentrate on the points which seem unusual and are immediately noticeable in contrast to other cultures. These are the issues that foreigners immediately call "typically German."

   - Culture standards are developed on the basis of general indications and do not describe the fine differentiations that exist between individuals and groups and the levels and sectors that exist in business and industry. Culture standards are unable to deal with reactionary, oppositional and socially critical behaviour, but rather concentrate mainly on the collective tendencies, which must be regarded as the predominant behavioural patterns. There are, of course, many aspects of German behaviour that are *not* mentioned in this book. They are ubiquitous and typical of many cultures and are therefore not particularly German. For example, Germans are not just task-orientated; they are also aware of the positive effect emotional expression and a good relationship can have on the work environment. Nevertheless, the striking point here is that Germans are significantly more task-orientated than people from other cultures, and will remain committed to this orientation. Consequently, the German culture standard *"Objectivism"* describes this phenomenon exactly.

– The method of generating culture standards by asking Germans for explanations of their behaviour may occasionally be responsible for a slightly positive distortion. Thus the culture standards as explained by Germans interviewed for this book may be too positive and may contain a certain amount of projection on their part: they may be telling us about the way they would *like* to perceive their culture.

– These occasional positive distortions are unavoidable, but do not affect our overall concept of German culture standards because the information derived from the explanations given is still valid. After all, the German system of "ideal" culture standards as it is experienced, seen, taught and passed on, is still described and depicted truthfully. Therefore it provides non-Germans with what they must keep in mind and do in order to be accepted by Germans.

3. The description of German culture standards describes behaviour considered to be correct, decent, "OK," harmless and so on by Germans themselves. There are, of course, always situations where these culture standards will be intentionally ignored by certain individuals – when they do not care about social norms and just want to "do their own thing." This is almost always a personal issue and should not be used to make a generalisation about the whole of German society. This can take two forms: either a culture standard (for example, honesty, rule-oriented internalised control or one's responsibility to share and inform) is just not followed by the individual, or it is obeyed so strictly and the behaviour is taken to such extremes, that it negates the culture standard altogether.

An example of this would be when someone purposely takes advantage of German directness in order to intimidate or hurt another. You will not find any examples like this in this book. This kind of behavior is not typical and characteristic in any way. Most Germans are good-natured and strive very hard to make each cooperative working situation as successful as possible.

4. Culture standards form a cultural system through their interaction with one another. Thus only seldomly does a single culture standard sufficiently explain a critical incident, instead it must be seen in the light of the interplay of various culture standards. However, since I have a great many critical incidents to share in this volume, each one will function primarily as an illustration for a particular culture standard. I have chosen them because I feel they are good, typical examples of that particular culture standard and for this reason I discuss each one only once. The reader will be correct in thinking occasionally that some of the examples act as prototypes for a whole system of values.

5. My point of reference is mainly the business world. The people I have dealt with were predominantly academics, technicians and high-level managers, all of whom have had intercultural experience and/or lived as expatriates. I am convinced that my experiences and the results from the Regensburg Research Institute could be transferable into other work sectors such as migration, refugee work and military cooperation. This assumption, however, has yet to be tested and scientifically researched.

■ The Historical Context

Cultural Standards and Their Historical Genesis

It is easier to understand a person better when we know his or her life story and can see what has shaped that person in both a positive and a negative sense; namely the successes and the failures that have been endured. The same is true of nations: more light is shed on the primary characteristics of a nation if we look at its history. Both the individual characteristics of human beings and the collective characteristics of a nation are better explained by taking history into consideration. Culture standards have their roots in specific historical conditions: they evolved at some specific time or other and provided both logical answers to the questions and challenges of that time and an active way of responding within the collective, organized social fabric. Cultures tend to resemble one another more or less depending on how similar living conditions were.

Cultural standards have the tendency to change over the course of time, if the geohistorical conditions exert continual adaptive pressure. More recent developments only gradually – and incompletely – repress and replace existing culture standards (Dinzelbacher 1993), and this only occurs when older elements prove unsuitable and restrictive in the present context. The remains of the behaviour which have proven worthy of being kept are maintained unchanged or are adapted to the new conditions. To date no theory exists as to how this really happens (Raulff 1987), but it is certain that "mentality is what changes the slowest" (Le Goff 1987, p. 23). The rhythm of the rise and fall of cultural standards is therefore measured in generations and centuries. Thus, on the one hand, cultures have a marked continuity, whereas, on the other hand, they are in a constant process of change.

This becomes particularly obvious in the so-called history of ideas. The influence of Christianity as a system of ideas is not dependent on whether a particular individual is a practising Christian or not. Religion served as a framework for shaping the everyday life of many earlier generations whose behaviour was passed down to us even to this day, often without reference to the original Christian roots and intentions. Religious leaders throughout the centuries have concerned themselves with the diverse currents of reigning thought, so that each era contributed toward the further development of religion.

In this book I not only describe the German mentality but also try to trace the emergence of the current German culture standards. In this context I regard history like the history of the earth, the eras of which can be read in the different layers of rock; and I try to connect some important historical events (mainly cultural) with the empirical results in the behaviour of present day Germans. I tend to neglect the details: even the most recent history of two German states is nearly absent. I pursue only the directly relevant historical lines. This means both looking at recent changes and exposing older foundations. It is evident that most cultural standards have ancient roots, sometimes even in several spheres. It is this strong, over-determined nature that makes them very robust and "typically" German. Other European nations may have experienced the same eras more briefly or more intensely, or some other era may have more lastingly influenced their patterns of behaviour, or they may have completely escaped these experiences altogether, and so forth.

This historical perspective is a structure which has the drawbacks of being hypothetical and fragmentary in character. The assumptions and statements must only be seen as a *possible* or *probable* means of explanation which lay no claim to being verifiable. They are meant to be of a potential, plausible, comprehensible and discussible nature, a scenario for the development of values (Klages 1987). Here, I have followed the leads provided by several eclectic works by various authors in an attempt to depict critical periods that appear to have been decisive for certain culture standards. The consequent explanations cannot be seen as exhaustive but rather as part of the possible reasons for these cultural standards arising. This is all the more applicable since the findings on the history of mentality (in the sense of a mindset) are very sparse (Dinzelbacher 1993; Raulff 1987).

◼ Principal Eras of German History

The rise of the German people took centuries. The significant historical developments throughout this time took place in the Mediterranean region: in the development of Judaism, ancient Greek civilisation, during the Roman Empire, and in the church which christianised the north. The word "deutsch" (German) initially referred only to the language spoken in various dialects in the eastern part of the realm of Charlemagne. The western part comprised people speaking various Roman/Latin dialects. After the death of Charlemagne in 814, the empire fell apart and the political boundaries largely coincided with the language boundaries between the precursors of modern "France" and "Germany." Gradually the word "deutsch" (German) was transferred to the speakers of the dialects and ultimately to the territory itself.

The origin of the German Empire is usually dated from 911, when the Carolingian dynasty died out and the Franconian Duke Conrad I was elected King. The Empire was an electoral monarchy. There was no capital city: whilst roving through his realm, the King ruled at alternate locations. There were also no imperial taxes; instead the King drew his income from the imperial estates he administered in trust. The tribal Dukes were powerful and he could only command respect through military power and the skilful forging of alliances. The greatest expansion of power was gained by Otto I (936–973) who was recognised as King and was able to have himself crowned Emperor by the Pope in 952.

Empireship was in theory universal. The Emperor was meant to rule the whole Occident – which of course never became political reality – and he was the protector of the church, which linked the ecclesiastical infrastructure to the political events of the empire. Yet only rarely did it secure precedence over the papacy, which was quite contrary to the original intention. From this time on, all Kings had to make their way to the Pope in Rome in order to be crowned Emperor. This had the practical consequence that a great deal of energy was invested in Italian politics, which diverted the ruler from important tasks within the German empire. This soon led to heavy setbacks within the central power "Kingdom": In the 13th century the spiritual and worldly princes finally achieved the status of semi-sovereign princes. The strength within the German Empire was split, preventing the formation of a national state, which had already been forged in other Western European countries.

Territorial fragmentation took root in the German empire. The imperial estates were lost and, when Rudolf I (1273–1291) ascended to the throne, he had to secure his material basis from his own Habsburg dynasty. Thus "allodium politics" increasingly became every Emperor's main point of interest. The cities gained increasing influence thanks to their economic power. The imperial crown was practically bequeathed within the house of Habsburg. The imperial reforms (Imperial Diet, Imperial Counties, Imperial Court) ultimately remained ineffective. Other forces in the empire – the electors (allowed to elect the King), princes and cities – expanded their influence to the detriment of imperial power.

The top ecclesiastical rulers, for example Prince-Bishops, also interfered happily, whilst simultaneously an intellectual change characterised by Enlightenment and Humanism was occurring. The smouldering dissatisfaction with the church eventually led to the Reformation when Martin Luther appeared on the scene in 1517, and triggered an intellectual, and in part political, revolutionary movement. Nevertheless, both the uprising of the imperial knights as well as the Peasants' War failed, and the main beneficiaries were once again the Princes. After wide-spread battles they attained the right to dictate their subjects' religion in 1555, with the result that Germany eventually became four-fifths Protestant. The Catholic Church prepared its Counter-Reformation, the conflicts intensified, and Germany ultimately plunged into the Thirty Years War (1618–1648). This conflict expanded into a pan-European conflict of the superpowers of that time for supremacy in Europe, and by the time this conflict ceased, vast areas of Germany had been devastated and almost totally depopulated.

The Peace of Westphalia (1648) resulted in territorial loss, with Switzerland and the Netherlands leaving the empire. The approximately 360(!) remaining semi-sovereign regions on German territory retained their territorial rights and now began to practise an absolutist form of government based on the French model: the ruler wielded limitless power, introduced tight administration, fiscal policy and standing armed forces. Many Princes also wanted to transform their residences into cultural centers, and representatives of "enlightened absolutism" promoted the sciences and art in their territories. A mercantilist economic policy strengthened some states economically. As allodium of the Habsburg family, Austria became a multinational state and rose to great power, whilst Prussia became a military power under Frederick the Great (1740–1786). The Empire now existed for all intents and purposes only as an idea and on paper.

When the Revolution broke out in France in 1789, the failed attempt by Austria and Prussia to intervene in the neighbouring country to defend the feudal social order triggered a counter-attack by the Napoleonic revolutionary armies. In 1806 Emperor Franz II abdicated. The "Holy Roman Empire of German Nation" ceased to exist. The French Revolution itself did not spread to Germany because the federal structure strongly resisted expansion and revolutionary France still constituted a foreign and occupational power in the eyes of most Germans. The ideas spawned in France definitely led to some reforms (abolition of serfdom, freedom of trade, municipal self-administration, equality before the law and military service), although the right of citizens to legislative participation was still denied in many states. After the victory over Napoleon, the Congress of Vienna re-drew the map of Europe in 1814/15 but a free, united nation-state of Germany was still not created. The German Confederation was only a loose association of individual sovereign states which monitored the status quo in a reactionary fashion (Restoration). The attempt to establish a constitutional monarchy in the St. Pauls Church in Frankfurt in 1848 also failed.

Meanwhile, modern economic development had taken root, with the railway system, industrialisation, and a substantial economic upswing in the 1850s. Prussia advanced to economic predominance within Germany. Bismarck, the Prime Minister of Prussia, worked intensively to achieve German unity (without Austria, which had already insisted on its own multinational state in 1848) and conquered France in the Franco-German War of 1870/71. King William I of Prussia was subsequently proclaimed the German Emperor. The Germans entered world history as a "latecomer nation" with a belated national unity. Although Bismarck pursued a far-sighted foreign policy, and passed various social laws, he was opposed to domestic democratic tendencies. In any case, Emperor William II continued to think in monarchist terms and eventually dismissed Bismarck to rule on his own.

Although the question of blame for the outbreak of World War I

(1914–1918) remains controversial, its result is a hard fact: the military defeat of the German Empire simultaneously meant its political collapse, and in 1918 the Emperor and the Princes abdicated. Germany was declared a republic and a parliamentary democracy.

The Weimar Republic was a "republic without republicans," fought against by its opponents and only half-heartedly defended by its supporters. In particular the ensuing postwar economic misery, the dire lack of democratic tradition and the horrendous level of reparations contained in the Peace Treaty of Versailles contributed to the problems of this emerging democracy. The result was instability and the decline of the Republic beginning with the world economic crisis in 1929. At the elections to the Reichstag in 1932, Hitler's National Socialist Party became the most powerful political force in the country and, in 1933, Hitler was elected Chancellor. He immediately secured almost unlimited authority for himself (the Enabling Acts), persecuted political opponents and minorities, suppressed freedom of speech and set up a racist dictatorship that eventually led to the Second World War (1939–1945). After capitulation in May 1945, Germany was divided into British, French, American and Russian occupation zones. The Federal Republic of Germany was established in 1949 in the three Western zones, and the German Democratic Republic subsequently in the Soviet occupation zone. These two Germanies soon found themselves separated by the so-called iron curtain. Following political changes throughout the Eastern bloc, 1990 saw the re-unification of the two German states.

But how has the history of the Germans, as briefly outlined here, shaped the mentality of its people? A survey of opinions by authors who have dealt with just this question provides the following thoughts:

1. The pillars of Western civilization, *classical antiquity* and *Judeo-Christian religion* as well as the teachings of *Protestantism* and its consequences, deeply and lastingly shaped social life. Protestantism led to a unique epoch of German national history, which although it constituted a "revolution," sealed the fragmentation of Germany by religiously sanctified bloodshed.

2. The disintegration of the authority kept the people within the confines of *territorial states* with an absolutist state system for centuries. The multitude of small state structures tended to limit the horizon of the majority of the people within them and frequently

led to interstate rivalry and disputes, some of which ended in social catastrophes.

3. The continuous *existential upheavals* which continue to plague generations of Germans up to this day have instilled large sections of the population with a feeling of powerlessness albeit without destroying their inherent interest in state affairs.

I describe these historical developments and eras in greater detail in the context of the historical roots of each individual culture standard.

To the point!

Central German Culture Standards

Objectivism

How Germans are perceived by other cultures	
well-qualified specialists, competent within their fields	*Brazilians, Indonesians, Russians, Taiwanese*
qualifications are important – they study for a long time	*British*
"cold" thinking, logic has a higher priority than emotion and mercy	*Spanish, Hungarians*
rational, sensible	*British, Hungarians*
logical – they always have a reason for what they do	*Japanese*
being objective (technology and economics) is more important than the feelings one has for something	*French*
direct – they come straight to the point	*Taiwanese*
do not ask their business partners about private matters	*Portuguese*
even people in helping professions (e.g. doctors) remain distant and don't talk much	*French, Indians, US-Americans*
cars are treasured	*Finnish*
miserly, petty, thrifty with money	*British, Koreans, Hungarians, Czechs*

As an introduction to the following chapter let me re-tell a short story as it was told during an intercultural training session on Germany:

A German boss comes to a Brazilian expatriate who is working at the German headquarters of his company as the coordinator between the Brazilian subsidiary and the German headquarters. He wants to get some documentation from Brazil that was promised to him four weeks ago, but still hasn't arrived. As his German boss enters the room, the Brazilian employee greets him in a friendly manner and starts a conversation about the weekend and yesterday's football match. After this exchange of pleasantries, the German boss makes it perfectly clear that he isn't interested in the employee's small-talk and breaks in with: "Let's talk business! I need the study on. . ." and he again summarises the contents of the desired documentation and states why he really needs it as soon as possible. The Brazilian tries once more to engage his boss in a friendly chat. The German boss ends this chat as quickly as it started by pronouncing once again that he is waiting for the documentation. He needs it urgently for his customer. As he picks up the phone, the Brazilian employee says, "In order to get the documentation, I have to make a call to Brazil." The boss now is breathing hard and audibly: "You haven't gotten it yet? – Typical for a Brazilian!" The Brazilian employee, who in the meantime has managed to get his Brazilian colleague on the line, is having a polite chat with her about the weather, how she's feeling and so on. While this is going on, the German boss is waiting impatiently and getting more annoyed. "I have a little problem," the Brazilian employee tells his colleague after a while. "I need the documentation. My German boss is in my office right now and is waiting for it." "No problem," says the colleague from the Brazilian office, "I can fax it to you, then you'll have it in a minute." Sure enough the fax soon starts printing out the long-awaited documentation. The German boss picks up the fax with a sarcastic comment: "Great! And I had to wait four weeks for this!" and stalks out of the office.

Whenever people meet, they meet on at least two different levels: on the *task level* which deals with content and is objective, and on the *social-emotional level* which deals with individual emotions and relationships. We meet on the task level when we meet as professionals, trying to achieve work-related goals. The social-emotional level is characterised by the atmosphere or relationship between the people meeting and their perception of one another as, for example, nice, arrogant or unfriendly. Cultural differences occur in meetings when one person's culture may place more emphasis on the task level to understand what is happening, whereas the other person's culture sees the social-emotional level as more important. Both levels are important to both cultures, but to different degrees. In the workplace, Germans are well-known for preferring to stay on the task level: a central German culture standard is this objectivity and task-orientation. The effect of German objectivity and task-orientation can now be seen in the earlier story about the Brazilian:

The Brazilian is quite irritated by his boss's behaviour, but at the same time, he wonders what may have caused it. He feels the German's behaviour was very aggressive from the beginning– and then got even more so. The boss wasn't even a tiny bit friendly, not even for a second; he didn't attempt to make small talk, he didn't share or show anything of his personality or demonstrate any interest in anything other than getting the documentation he had demanded. His whole manner of talking and interacting were frighteningly direct and pointed to the bewildered Brazilian. Furthermore, once he got what he wanted, the boss didn't even take the time to thank the friendly colleague in Brazil. In short, the Brazilian has no desire to work for a person like this. In the future, he won't give his boss anything and tell him anything unless specifically asked to do so, because he believes that such a person is not fit to be a boss.

Definition of Objectivism

When Germans work together professionally, the project or task at hand, the roles and the professional competence of the individuals involved are the central points. The motivation to cooperate results from the need to meet the demands of a situation. In business meetings Germans remain objective. They "get to the point" and they "stick to the point." Being "objective" is a highly esteemed characteristic of German "professionalism": Germans present themselves as being goal-oriented and as people who support their contributions to discussions and arguments with facts. They enter meetings well-prepared. They often bring written materials that can be very detailed. Such preparation is done in order to create the basis for an objective discussion and mutual cooperation. Germans value the written word, because only then are the agreements, rules or facts clearly recorded in black and white, without the distraction of vague chatter. If the people involved, for example in a business deal, know each other well or find that they like each other this is seen as a pleasant side-effect, but it is not a matter of primary importance. For this reason, Germans put little effort into getting to know their business partners or creating a friendly atmosphere. The objectives are the centre points of interest and everything else revolves around them. Regardless of all else, the goals and the tasks at hand have top priority.

To illustrate the meaning of these statements, here are a few observations that foreigners have made about Germans and their behaviour.

A Spanish colleague often travels home for vacation. During his last stay, he bought a box of Spanish wine to give to his German colleagues as gifts. Back in the office, he says to one of his German colleagues, "Here's some Spanish wine for you to try. It is a little present from me." The German colleague seems to be completely surprised and asks, "This is for me? Really? Why?" "Yes, it's for you. It's just a little present. No reason." The German seems almost embarrassed by the present, and sheepishly murmurs a few words of gratitude. The Spaniard goes to the next colleague and also gives him a bottle of wine. This colleague seems to be equally surprised and says, "Well, that's nice. But why?" The friendly Spaniard decides to take the third bottle of Spanish wine back to his apartment. He doesn't dare to give out any more wine to his colleagues because he has the impression that he has, more than anything else, embarrassed his colleagues when all he wanted to do was to be nice to them.

An English engineer is the head of a department in a German company. A deadline is drawing closer and closer and time is running out, so he asks his employees to come in to the office to work on a Saturday, so they can complete the job on time. All of them show up (and are paid, by the way, the normal overtime pay according to their contracts). On Monday, the British department head goes around to all of those who had worked on Saturday and thanks them. Furthermore, he tells them that they have done a good job, that he is very satisfied with their performance and that he has already been able to send the work out on time to the customer. His colleagues look at him in obvious surprise and seem to be a bit astounded by his behaviour.

A British expatriate living in Germany notices that at the end of a phone call, Germans always put down the receiver rather abruptly without exchanging some polite small talk to finish off a conversation. Germans say something like: "Okay, we'll meet tonight at 6:00 p. m., Goodbye" – and then they immediately hang up. He racks his brain as to how he can be quicker than the Germans on the other end of the line. He tries keeping his finger on the cradle, so that he can push it as soon as the conversation has ended, but hasn't yet succeeded in being quicker to end the conversation than the Germans he has spoken with.

Although these different situations portray many facets, they all have one central point in common: all of the Germans are acting on the objective or task level and have relegated all social-emotional aspects of communication to a secondary level:

- The boss wants the documentation from Brazil, he doesn't want to chat!
- Relationships among colleagues are largely defined by the nature of the work (objective and task-oriented) and are mostly limited to the workplace. Giving each other gifts is easily seen as a "transgression" of social rules, unless there is a special reason for it (for example, a birthday or marriage).
- An employee's obligation to work on Saturdays is contractually settled and is not seen as a personal favour to the head of the department, so that there is no expectation that he should specially thank them for it.
- When everything has been said, the phone call is over. Why beat around the bush and ramble on?

In all of these examples, Germans definitely appreciate the "human" side of the situation, but they would never *expect* it, or see it to be of primary importance. From a German point of view, what they have done is totally sufficient, because they have met the objective demands of the situation. The friendliness of others might be nice, but it is not necessary: the friendliness of the Brazilian employee could even be seen as a way of distracting his boss from the unfinished work.

The Objective as the Focal Point

In business encounters, Germans place the highest priority on the specific objective of the interaction: bankers on money, developers on technical engineering matters, purchasers on the price and in transportation and logistics it is placed on the planning. All organisational measures and most of the interactions between people have the goal of allowing all persons involved to be able to work with one another on an objective and task-oriented level.

When colleagues meet– even those from different companies– they meet because of their specific roles and professional qualifications. Collaborating with others does not necessarily mean establishing a social relationship with them beforehand. The persons involved interact on the basis of their roles and responsibilities and meet to discuss matters, even if they do not know each other well or at all. Because Germans trust that their colleagues or partners in business interactions have been carefully selected based on the demands of the project at hand, they do not initially question that competence.

The concentration that Germans invest in the task at hand and on fulfilling the role they have in the workplace can often be so extreme that any signals unrelated to these objective matters are not noticed or are ignored:

An Italian-German joint venture is about to be established, requiring many business meetings between the Italian and German partners. Sometime during one of the meetings, one of the Italian managers suggests, in a side remark, that they could go skiing together next winter, but none of the Germans pay much attention. In March, the German CEO's Secretary receives a phone call from Italy. The ski weekend is set for two weeks from now. A hotel in the Dolomites has already been reserved, but now they need to know how many people from the German office will be coming. The German CEO is quite surprised (to be honest, he has completely forgotten the Italian's suggestion) but feels obliged to respond positively. He sends a letter to everyone in the company, saying that he would like as many employees as possible to go skiing. A positive response comes from the German company's ski club, as well as from a few other employees, who find the idea of skiing in Italy quite tempting. The result is that a bus full of a diverse mixture of German employees, brought together by their interest in skiing, arrives in the Dolomite ski resort. Upon arrival they are completely embarrassed when they are greeted by the *very* top-level Italian managers! The Italians are obviously quite surprised that only one of the managers they met at the joint venture meetings gets off the bus. Nevertheless the Italians are friendly and hospitable: they have reserved a wonderful slope for the skiers and have organised a tournament. The dinner celebrating the event is magnificent.

The Germans certainly didn't want to offend the Italians. They simply failed to take into consideration that the future success of their joint venture could be (or from the Italian point of view *must* be) dependent on the relationships built up between the managers.

The management style of German executives is above all, task-oriented. A boss generally limits his interactions with his employees to business related themes. "Hands on," personal management is rather uncommon. If there are things to discuss, people arrange a meeting.

Otherwise the employees, like the boss, are so focussed on their responsibilities and tasks at hand that they are unlikely to have or take the time to chat. German bosses insist on the importance of fulfilling duties, formulating plans, developing structures, meeting deadlines and showing competencies. This is what they say they want, this is their goal in a discussion, and when necessary, this is what they put pressure on their employees to show that they are capable of, and this is how performance is ultimately evaluated. German bosses are, after all, responsible for the successful completion of specific objectives. The employees are the "tools" needed to achieve the company's goals and their work must therefore be properly coordinated.

A boss has the right to give orders to his team, although many bosses, especially those with more modern attitudes towards leadership, try to lead their staff by convincing them (participatory management style). This is why employees, especially those from India and East Asia, are often dumbfounded when they observe that even considerable differences in seniority can be put aside in discussions for the sake of the task at hand and that everyone discusses the matter as if they had equal status within the company hierarchy.

The manager of the distribution department of a Chinese textile manufacturer is holding a meeting with his Chinese and German team leaders. He informs them of the orders coming up in the near future and assigns them individual tasks. Whilst the Chinese employees accept their tasks without complaint, promising to do their best, the German team leaders react quite differently. They completely reject some of the bosses' ideas because they believe they are impractical. The Chinese manager is surprised by this behaviour and tries to convince them with explanations, but even after a long discussion and the evaluation of several options, the Germans still insist on their point of view, which leaves the Chinese manager at a complete loss. He wonders whether the Germans' rejection of his orders is directed against him and/or if they have lost interest in maintaining the relationship with him that up until now has been very good.

An Indian engineer is currently working in production at a German site. During a meeting, one of his German colleagues applies for a wireless phone since he is often away from his desk somewhere in the production area. The Indian holds his breath: nobody has a wireless phone, not even their boss! How could his German colleague dare to ask for one? Their boss, who is German, listens carefully to the reasons that the German colleague gives for needing this phone and to the Indian's astonishment, approves the request. Shortly afterwards the desired telephone arrives. The Indian asks himself how this can be possible in Germany.

Another Indian engineer is also working in production in Germany. Since new software will have to be installed in the near future, several meetings have taken place in which the different features of this software are discussed. The boss is visibly taking pains to listen attentively to his employees and at the same time to express his opinions in a convincing manner in the hope of winning them over to his strategy for dealing with the software installation. Different opinions are expressed and discussion continues until a consensus is reached. In short: the boss discusses the situation with his subordinates on a cooperative level. In the Indian's opinion, the decision that the boss makes in the end is not really his own but rather one made collectively. The Indian is completely unused to such behaviour from his Indian bosses.

Experts are held in high esteem in Germany. What they say is taken seriously, and in business dealings their opinions are carefully looked at and taken into consideration. The status of being an expert is clearly defined by facts: someone who has profound knowledge in a particular field. Whether this person is socially skilled or has useful social contacts, whether this person has personality, charm or charisma is irrelevant to their title of "expert." Expert status is achieved through academic study and the qualification and title that come with it. This gives the expertise a label (for example, Bachelor of Engineering, Master of Business Administration or even a Doctorate), and also shows what level of expertise the person has reached, which is important for job chances and promotion. German administrative and organisational systems, even where people are being organised, are often impersonal and objectified. Computerised data management is based on facts, numbers and data which can be collected, stored and manipulated. Supervision of employees and their performance in person by close and regular contact is uncommon in Germany. There is an expectation that problem analysis and solutions based on computer generated data is effective and motivating.

In many German companies managers are clearly focussed on performance and objective data. The social atmosphere of the company is of secondary importance – that is, unless the company's performance hints at relationship problems amongst employees. The number one concern of German business people is money. Costs, margins and profits are the factors Germans often refer to when it comes to making decisions and also when conflicts need to be resolved. Cost/benefit equations are extremely important to them and for this reason they often make decisions based on the costs involved and if it is worthwhile. This concern with money is often perceived negatively by non-Germans as an exaggerated form of thriftiness or even greed.

Another aspect of the German culture standard of a focus on tasks, facts and objects can be seen in the high value Germans place on personal property. People take great care of their cars, homes and gardens. The possessions of others are also respected. Financial matters are taken seriously, even when small sums of money are involved. Material possessions are seen as part of a person's private life, which is why it is rather unusual to lend them out in an easy-going way. All of these unspoken social rules even apply amongst good friends. Generally, the lasting joy of acquiring and possessing material objects is preferred to more fleeting pleasures.

Communication Style

A Spanish controller working in Germany and a group of his Spanish friends are talking to a group of German colleagues. Somehow the topic of conversation turns to the city traffic. The Germans openly and without embarrassment criticise the poorly planned city road system. The Spaniard is astounded at how objectively the Germans speak their mind. They describe the situation so clearly, with no attempt to gloss over the problem or "paint a prettier picture" for the benefit of the Spaniards. Being able to look at things clearly and objectively is obviously normal and important to the Germans.

Business communication generally stays on the objective level. It stays within the agreed upon boundaries and focusses on the common goal. Germans take pains to present the facts and their significance as objectively as possible, making many a presentation extremely dry, to say the least. The German style of communication can be so fact-oriented and objective that the "human" level is all but lost.

The objective way Germans present facts can be perceived as offensive, especially when there is a problem and they start to relentlessly analyse all of the weak spots. The so-called "soft factors," or human sensitivities, are often ignored; hurts and insults go unnoticed or are seen as unavoidable, "a professional must be able to cope with criticism and argument – it's part of the job."

A German engineer has a meeting with a French colleague to discuss certain aspects of the product design for a customer's order. The French engineer suggests installing solar panels on the roof of the car, because in the customer's country the sun would be shining most of the time. The German engineer agrees with his colleague that the suggestion is basically a good idea, but not feasible because: a) the solar panels would have to be cleaned regularly in order to keep working, and b) oil would have to be used on the vehicle's roof, which would probably cause problems. Both of these innovations would greatly increase the maintenance on the customer's part, and as far as the German engineer can judge from previous business dealings he has had with this customer, the customer is unlikely to accept this. Furthermore, if the maintenance were neglected, then the whole thing would have to be scrapped as an expensive mistake. The discussion of the pros and cons goes back and forth between the two colleagues. Two days later, the German engineer receives an e-mail from his French colleague, addressed to his boss with a copy to him. The email contains the minutes of their meeting and indicates that the German was uncooperative. The German engineer is very surprised: in his eyes, he had only made objective comments about the problems connected with putting the French engineer's ideas into practice!

A German company has recently established a subsidiary in the Czech Republic. There are many problems. The German manager observes his Czech employees closely. He oversees how often they visit their clients and together with them he analyses their work, "Why aren't we successful? How can we improve our performance?" Many shortcomings are found; some of them solvable, and some of them not because circumstances do not allow for radical change at present. One breakthrough is finding the causes of many serious problems affecting one customer in particular. Last year, the Czech branch recorded a loss, but this will be made up for this year with a profit. This analysis of the problems, as difficult and threatening as it was for the Czech employees in the beginning, has turned out to be to their benefit. Positive changes are already beginning to take place. Now they can meet with their German boss without fear, but it has taken them a long time to get used to his style of communication and problem solving.

In business meetings Germans are direct because they want to achieve their goals. They do not waste time with niceties, but come straight to the point. They concentrate on the things that seem relevant to them; side-tracking, small talk or the time-consuming establishment of contacts on a personal level is simply considered a waste of time.

If Germans have set their mind on winning someone over to one of their goals or ideas, they thoroughly prepare their arguments in order to convince the other person. This means concentrating on the facts: conditions, requirements and consequences of any negotiation are clearly stated. Only after the facts and the logic behind them have been made perfectly clear do Germans start to think of switching to the social-emotional level, perhaps by allowing humour to come into the conversation or by making a personal remark. Proving their competence by their presentation of the facts allows them to switch from a professional to a personal level.

When it comes to decisions and making deals in which there are both objective points and a personal element, Germans inevitably stress the objective aspects. From the German point of view, it is seen as a sign of weakness to place too much importance on the subjective, or the personal, feeling side when making a decision. Whatever makes the most sense is right and is given top priority. Personal feelings can, at best, take the back seat and be seen faintly in the final decision.

When Germans make excuses, they tend to refer to facts which may be true, but somehow miss the mark. Excuses relating to personal problems or situations are only accepted in exceptional cases.

Not only at work, but also in every day life, public discussions and conversations are focussed on objective and impersonal topics at the expense of more personal matters. In this way, conversations *can* be critical examinations about the particular fact-related, objective topic at hand.

An American is always having the same unpleasant experience. Germans he has just become acquainted with start talking with him in a very critical way about the USA: the poor treatment of Afro-Americans, the disadvantages of the two party system, American military operations abroad, the high crime rates in big American cities and so on. He often feels under personal attack during these conversations, and sometimes gets hurt and defensive. Furthermore, he is astonished that Germans start talking about such serious matters with him when they hardly even know his name. He finds these situations very uncomfortable and more often than not doesn't know how to react. On the one hand, he is well aware of the problems mentioned, but on the other hand he doesn't want to take on the role of defending the United States.

Objective information gives Germans a yardstick against which to measure themselves and others: people define themselves mainly by their tasks and their achievements. Even in the interactions of every day life, emotions are kept under control. This is why many foreigners from cultures in which personal and social relationships are allowed to come to the fore (for example, Indians and Hungarians), often find discussions with Germans boring. They miss the personal element; the human touch.

The German colleagues of an Englishman spend the lunch break talking about their recent purchases of things for around the house. Each of them seems to be a specialist: the pros and cons of different tools and appliances are discussed in great detail, and the prices of different shops and hardware stores are compared to each other. One of the German colleagues has subscribed to the magazine of "Stiftung Warentest" (produced by a German consumer organisation) and therefore always knows the essential criteria for choosing what to buy. The Englishman finds these detailed and earnest discussions laughable. He himself is neither willing nor able to take part. However, since he is thinking of buying a new TV, he asks his German colleagues for their recommendations. The next day, they come prepared with various brochures and test results and suggest a particular TV, which he buys.

In summary, Germans have a tendency to talk about things which interest them on the objective level much more than they talk in order to build and nurture relationships. Accordingly, small-talk is often seen as exhausting, pointless and a sheer waste of time.

The Objective Level and the Subjective Level

Both the objective (task) level and the subjective (social-emotional) level play an important role in personal encounters. It is therefore important to understand how Germans attempt to come to grips with these two very different levels. Germans are decidedly objective and task-oriented in their approach to work, but they also use this objective level as a way into a more personal type of interaction on a social-emotional level.

- In the German professional context, mutual trust is established when two people cooperate well on a task. If the cooperation is fruitful, the partners involved have proven themselves to be trustworthy.
- Germans show themselves to be well-prepared, competent and experts in their field. This allows their partners to respect and value them and provides motivation for future cooperation. The seeds for a positive personal relation have been sown.

- Germans expect colleagues to share a great deal of information (relevant facts, data, figures, background information) from the first day of any collaboration to the last. It is quite normal for them to virtually flood their partners with information, usually in written form. By offering their complete repertoire of know-how to their partners and making themselves completely available, they are sending a signal on the social-emotional level that they are more than willing to cooperate.
- If problems arise, Germans will demonstrate that they are in command and will analyse the problem thoroughly. They invest time and energy in solving the problems. This demonstrates that they are committed and deserve respect, just as they respect colleagues who are similarly professional, and this is how a good relationship between colleagues is maintained.
- A collaboration has been going on for years, during which time a group of German colleagues has been intent on achieving success. There has been no lessening in their enthusiasm and dedication to the tasks at hand and the long-term goals. All the signs of a long-term, reliable relationship are there.
- The content and the formulation of an agreement make it clear, who is respected and why, and how deeply they are trusted.
- Changes in concepts and plans – even if demanded by the circumstances – are not only of importance on the objective task-level, they also threaten the relationship between colleagues, because of the additional work and inconvenience they can cause. Changes that occur on account of personal problems or circumstances need to be explained and apologised for, with thanks for the other person's understanding and acceptance of the situation. Should the need for change be announced in advance, it is made clear throughout the discussion and implementation process that the existing good relationship is valued and should continue.

This also works the other way around: anyone who disappoints others on the objective task level cannot expect a good relationship on the personal level. In the worst-case scenario, any attempt to be friendly may even be interpreted as a calculated strategy to cover up mistakes instead of wanting to correct them (as in the example of the Brazilian and the long-promised documentation). Anyone who enters a professional situation unprepared will not earn respect and has no chance of developing positive relationships. Anyone who tries to squirm their way out when troubles arise is deserting not just their responsibilities but also their colleagues. Anyone who is not fully committed obviously does not think that the collaborative relationship with their colleagues is particularly important. Anyone who changes plans without due thought and consultation shows a complete lack of consideration for colleagues and their well-being.

When Germans are disappointed on a personal level with a colleague, they suddenly stop being focussed and objective and instead openly show their annoyance and hurt. This sudden change can be perplexing for foreign colleagues. The reason for this sudden change is that both the professional objective level and the social-emotional level are inseparable: Germans define their professional relationships according to the commitment their colleagues show on the objective level to tasks and goals, though this is never openly said. The weight that each level carries remains the same: the task at hand always has the highest priority, even when it is clear that other things are also important.

Advantages and Disadvantages of the Culture Standard "Objectivism"

The advantage of focussing on tasks is that it provides the clear and direct means to achieving goals. Everything that might get in the way of this, including individual feelings and sensitivities, is ignored for the benefit of the task at hand.

Nevertheless, there are a number of disadvantages in this approach. The personal side of relationships suffers under the strain of this strict and harsh-seeming adherence to objectivity (see also the description of the culture standard *"Rule-Oriented, Internalised Control"*). As much as this behaviour is applauded for helping to achieve ambitious goals, it is nevertheless the cause of many problems on the personal level in relationships. This is especially true when decisions are made and action is expected because of the objective demands of the situation, without consideration of the fact that they will have a detrimental effect on a person's well-being.

A seminar is taking place in the Hungarian production plant of a German company, when a German working in the production department storms into the room without knocking. He doesn't greet anyone, but instead rudely interrupts the seminar leader who is speaking and shouts, "I desperately need five people right now to help me carry something out of the storage rooms!" He loudly calls out the names of five people and demands that they come with him. These people are clearly annoyed and for a short time they are torn between staying in the room and leaving, but they decide to go as ordered. The leader of the seminar and the other participants are left totally perplexed.

The German in this example was under extreme stress because production was about to come to a standstill. His reaction to the crisis was direct and task-oriented to the point that he broke all rules of acceptable conduct, even by German standards.This could be seen as exceptional behaviour were it not for the fact that it happens far too regularly to be ignored. In German production sites, there is a saying that "pressure is building up!" – "Druck aufbauen!" which signals, "Alarm! Come quickly!"

Occasionally, the focus on tasks and goals can be a cover-up for a hidden agenda, with many powerful emotions remaining hidden beneath seemingly objective arguments. At times, a lengthy and intense business meeting is in fact the outward manifestation of a raging but hidden power struggle. In Germany, people rarely steal the show in a funny, charming or openly disinterested way, rather, they do this by being critical, superior or cunning. Alternatively, in situations where emotions or subjective thoughts are the real motivation for decisions or actions, people avoid openly admitting this; instead finding objective arguments (which may of course actually exist). Some Germans compensate for their personal weaknesses and problems by focussing exclusively on facts, tasks, results and other objective areas. In all of these cases, regardless of how the people involved try to hide it, it is really emotions which are the key behavioural motivation. Because Germans resort to the objective level regardless of what they are fighting for or about, it is impossible to tell from their behaviour what their real motivation is; in fact they themselves may not even know.

An important decision has to be made about interactions: if they really are about objective things, behaviour can also be interpreted on the objective level. If, however, this objective approach is just a pretext, the real core of the matter may only come out with time, and little real progress will be able to be made on the objective level.

Despite the exceptions I have described here, it is true to say that

Germans are more often objective and task-oriented in their approach to work and life than non-Germans would ever suspect. Since the task level has priority over the social-emotional level, effort is always invested in dealing properly with it.

In intercultural encounters involving Germans and people from cultures which are more oriented towards a closer, more personal style of interaction the following vicious cycle can develop: the less success non-Germans have in establishing a good personal relationship, the harder they try. This behaviour in turn makes the Germans feel even more obstructed in their wish to "get to the point" and they start impatiently putting pressure on their non-German partners. This leads the non-Germans to invest *even more* effort into trying to establish a good personal relationship, which in turn makes the Germans more determinedly impersonal and objective. In the end, everyone is disappointed: the Germans by what they see as their colleagues' "unprofessionalism" and the non-Germans by the "coldness" of the Germans. This happens despite the fact that all concerned are struggling to achieve the basis for successful cooperation; namely, an interaction based on both the social-emotional and objective, task-oriented levels of communication.

A plane has landed in Naples, but the luggage of one passenger, a German businesswoman, has been taken to Milan by mistake. The German businesswoman goes to the lost luggage office and is quite upset, because she has absolutely nothing with her and the next plane from Milan to Naples is tomorrow morning. The Italian official is friendly, offers her a seat and a cup of coffee and listens to her attentively while she reports the mishap with her luggage. The Italian grows calmer and calmer during the course of the conversation and tries to placate the German by saying, "Calm down. We'll bring your luggage to your hotel as soon as it arrives. It will surely arrive on the next flight!" This upsets the German businesswoman even more. She just wants her suitcase, not a coffee and definitely not a soothing conversation! Now the boss comes into the lost luggage office and asks her about her plans in Naples; how long she intends to stay, and if she has been to Naples before and so on. "Why is he going on and on wasting my time?" the German businesswoman thinks to herself. The luggage office boss recommends taking a stroll through Naples. He, too, remains quite calm. "You have a reservation for a very good hotel. You will not lack for anything there. The hotel staff will take care of you." All of this upsets the businesswoman more and more. Finally, the Italian recommends the best shops in Naples. The German businesswoman is still angry, but thinks to herself that shopping for new clothes is probably the only thing she can do right now, as she does not want to wear jeans to tomorrow's business meeting. She is really annoyed and does not feel that her problem is really being taken seriously by the Italians. A little small-talk seems to be their way of getting themselves out of the mess they have made! She goes shopping. The next day, her suitcase is delivered to her hotel. Furthermore, she finds a note telling her to send the bills for her new clothes to the airline. Because of the regrettable inconvenience they have caused her they wish to compensate her by paying for her new clothes. Because she was so obsessed with her missing luggage and the consequences for tomorrow's conference, she hadn't noticed how nice the Italians had actually been or how they had tried to help her in her terrible situation.

To avoid any misunderstandings, let me repeat once more: of course, Germans have emotions just like everyone else. Because emotions exist in all cultures, it is not their presence in German behaviour that is particularly noticeable to non-Germans, but rather their *absence*– or the fact that they are "blocked out" in many situations where concentration is clearly on the objective tasks. This is, in short, what this chapter has been about.

Recommendations

Suggestions for non-Germans Working with Germans
- Be prepared for your German colleagues to remain focussed on the tasks and interact in an objective manner. If you don't expect anything different, you won't be disappointed.
- On the other hand, don't assume that this objective, task orientation is the *only* characteristic of Germans (refer, for example, to the culture standard *"Separation of Personality and Living Spheres"*).
- If you want to convince Germans of something or win them over to your view, be prepared to present your arguments and issues on the objective level. Be open to problem analysis and don't forget to present the points that are important and decisive in supporting your opinion. Carefully think through your arguments, find objective points that support your view, present them in a logical order and support them with facts. This will make Germans really listen to you, engage seriously in a conversation or discussion, and value you as a colleague. Subjective opinions or guesses are considered by Germans to be very unprofessional.

- If you wish to discuss "touchy-feely" social-emotional issues, then it is best if you support your cause from a platform that is as objective as possible. Plan ahead which points you could use to support your arguments as concretely and factually-based as possible. Often it is very useful to quantify any objective aspects and calculate any estimates or prognoses as realistically as possible.
- Generally speaking, if you wish to convince Germans of something, use data, facts and objective argumentation. Subjective opinions don't go over very well.
- Be aware that the objective task is the means that Germans use to establish relationships. Try to perceive the signals that are offered and to accept them as a gesture of wanting to start a relationship.
- Take advantage of everything that comes your way that could help you come in contact with Germans, even objective task-oriented issues. For example, ask for assistance if you wish to buy a car or some technical device or appliance (German men, in particular, are often experts in these fields), discuss your travel plans and talk about interesting places to visit in your own country (Germans love to travel), or speak about what you do in your free time (everyone has a hobby, you will certainly find something you like).

Suggestions for Germans Working with non-Germans
- Be aware of the fact that it is exactly this German culture standard – objective task-orientation – that is often perceived as being unfriendly and supports the stereotype of Germans being cold, inaccessible, arrogant and even aggressive.
- Try to enhance your objective, task-oriented behaviour by including more person-oriented social-emotional elements. Show yourself to be a human being with an individual personality, talk about personal matters and show your interest in your colleagues on this level too. Your colleagues from person-oriented cultures are equally interested in reaching good objective results; however, they don't see much hope for this when the social-emotional side of a professional relationship is dysfunctional.
- This does not mean that you should use personal relationships like a tool! First of all, your colleagues will see through you very quickly, and secondly only sincere behaviour will have positive effects in the long run. Try to establish a sincere, non-superficial relationship with your colleagues that fits both your personality

and theirs. Look for things that you may have in common. If you are unable to find any shared issues or interests with your colleagues, it's better to remain neutral than to spoil it all by pretending to be friendly.

- If you don't have a connection with your colleagues as people, all the objective task-orientation in the world may be of no assistance. At the beginning of any collaboration try to establish a relationship on the personal social-emotional level and pursue the objective level with less intensity. Make room and set aside time in which personal relationships can be created and worked on. The best basis for positive interaction with colleagues from person-oriented cultures is to establish a certain level of familiarity, which can only occur by getting to know each other. The feeling that one is in good hands is not likely to come about by listening to long lists of all the products or the company's merits or by being flooded with detailed information, but rather it is during small-talk or group activities that trust can be built up. After having successfully established personal relationships, don't forget to keep them up and nurture them.

- If your non-German partners show an interest in your personal life and ask questions about it, or if they have "leaked" personal information about you to others, don't misinterpret this as proof of nosiness or even worse spying against you; rather try to see it as a sign of their interest and appreciation: an effort to prepare themselves to work with you.

- Invest the time and energy it takes to build a good solid relationship with the people you have to work with on a regular basis. This does not mean just after work, but always: whilst making small-talk or chatting *at work* as well as being friendly when talking about task-oriented issues.

- In the best-case-scenario, you should try to find an individual solution to problems on the objective level which both fits the situation and clearly takes into consideration the needs of your non-German colleagues and shows your appreciation of their performance. You will then be perceived as someone who respects their colleagues and not as someone who stubbornly follows their own agenda.

Historical Background

There is a fundamental orientation in Western societies toward the subject. This is associated with the Judeo-Christian tradition (Nipperdey 1991, Cahill 2000), the monotheism of which denuded the world of multiple Gods, thereby opening it to the technical and scientific interests of humans. In a monotheistic world there are no semi-divine beings to consider. Therefore people can, for example, safely build mills since there are no nymphs living in the stream. Only a monotheistic creator, untroubled by such things, can say: "Conquer the world," not in the sense of armies and territory, but in terms of understanding and knowledge.

Christianity, by way of its doctrine of redemption, further motivated people to performance and a rational way of life. Theology legitimised this approach and the Benedictines implemented it with their "Ora et labora" or "Prayer and Work" philosophy. The significant irrational elements found in the Middle Ages were subsequently strongly repressed during the epoch of Enlightenment in line with the push to deal with all problems of life in a purely intellectual manner as opposed to historical, authoritative and somehow mystical powers (Troeltsch 1925). The Enlightenment represented the transition to modernity in Europe and ever since has formed the basis for Western "objectivism" which is still valid today.

Objectivism is a global concept, especially visible in Westernised cultures, but in order to understand the particularly German variation, we must consider particular German conditions and developments.

In Germany *Protestantism* in Christianity played a major role. According to Mensching (1966) there was a removal of emotional and irrational elements from religious ceremonies within Protestantism. Protestantism lacks a cultish aspect, for instance in the form of worship or spiritual sacrifice. Religiousness moved instead progressively towards the intellectual plane and the search for understanding; towards finding answers to concrete problems and helping in the search for existential meaning (Nuss 1992). As a result, people related less passionately and more intellectually to religion, which over generations led to a clear emphasis on objectivity and rationality. In fact, modern Germany was largely moulded by theologians.

Furthermore, the Protestant ethic sees humans as having been placed by God in their professional position as well as in their personal; a position they must hold down and carry out to the best of their abilities (Molz 1994). This mind-set does not primarily focus on people but on contents. The Lutheran faith in particular, with its doctrine of two worlds, emphasised a separation of life-spheres, which eventually led to task-orientation (concentration on the task at hand) and toward a richness of spirit (the individual inner life).

Another line of argument emphasises the lengthy period in which *small German states* predominated, which for many citizens meant a stable social fabric and relative immobility. It also implied relationships that did not constantly have to be re-negotiated. Consequently, it was much easier to concentrate on (common) objectives or tasks (see Molz 1994).

In the following centuries, when absolutism in the small states brought bureaucracy to full bloom, objectivism was encouraged even further:

- Firstly, bureaucracy in its essence is not focussed on individuals but on the regulation of affairs and the settlement of matters. Because of the geographical, political and social confinement of the small German states this system flourished. The task-oriented and methodical functions of bureaucracy to the benefit of the state and the ruling class were also adopted by the military and the middle class. From this social basis the associated values and moral codes radiated out into broader society (Molz 1994).
- This development was again intensified following the founding of the German Empire (1871). Through the Prussian-led military victory the particularly well-developed Prussian bureaucratic system gained recognition beyond the boundaries of Prussia and ended up being copied throughout Germany. Furthermore, not only were the Prussian state institutions comprehensively bureaucratised, but also the more productive industries, which were held up as models. Bureaucracy appeared to be *the* success story, in effect saying, "Wherever the individual has his station in life, he has to execute his daily tasks impersonally, objectively, correctly and unemotionally. The task is more important than the working environment. . ." (Pross 1982, p. 46).

More recent history begins with the so-called zero hour of 1945, this being the most recent low point of *existential upheaval*. In an effort to explain the German mentality from an outside, or foreign perspective, Brigitte Sauzay writes, "The conflict between generations is in no other European country as pronounced as it is in Germany . . . The entire Nazi vocabulary had become unusable. All false enthusiasm was shied away from, all pathos avoided . . . The law of the day was restraint and practical sobriety . . . This is the way in which the Federal Republic presents itself today: tame, . . . boring, but admirable for its economic success and its political organisation. Not many Frenchmen know that an infinitely richer and more diverse Germany hides behind this façade . . .: a far more likeable Germany . . ." (Sauzay 1986 p. 67). The German author Klages places this sobriety in the emotional context of society after the war: "The material reconstruction . . .was, in this atmosphere of dull self-hatred, a form of release. Here was a task they could turn to again without constant confrontation with reproaches or feelings of guilt" (Klages 1987, p. 215). Life became centred on functionality and the predominant emotions of isolation and powerlessness could be banished into the background.

The period of reconstruction after the Second World War constituted the most recent major reinforcing wave of German *"Objectivism."* In West Germany, the home of the economic miracle, the interpretation of the market economy focussed once again on the "object." The heart of the market economy is profit maximisation based on "survival of the fittest," which consequently requires individuals to be largely subordinate to the accepted objective interests. This is also true with respect to the market economy. The desired economic upturn succeeded, economic stability was substantially maintained, and to Germans today the broad orientation towards the "object" is still part and parcel of their success formula.

Operating Instructions

■ Appreciation for Rules, Regulations and Structures

How Germans are perceived by other cultures	
fond of order, organised, systematic, very detail-oriented, like everything to be planned and under control	*Australians, Brazilians, British, Chinese, Czech, Finnish, French,Hungarians, Indians, Indonesians, Italians, Japanese, Koreans, Mexicans, Polish, Singaporeans, Spaniards, Russian and US-Americans*
there are directions, rules and regulations everywhere, no trust in the creative and improvisational skills of others	*Australians, Belgians, Brazilians, Chinese, Czech, Dutch, Finnish, Italians, Koreans, Mexicans, Polish, Spaniards, Swedish, Taiwanese, Turkish, and US-Americans*
bureaucracy everywhere (even at work) – severe, strict and tough	*Belgians, Brazilians, British, Chinese, Hungarians, Mexicans, Swedish, Spaniards, South Africans and US-Americans*
predictable, without surprises, boring	*Indians, Italians, Czechs, Hungarians*
inflexible, stubborn, resistant to new ideas	*Brazilians, Chinese, British, French, Indians, Japanese, Koreans, Swedes, Spanish, Turks, US-Americans*
keen to correct others, know-it-alls	*Finns, French, Singaporeans, Spanish*
environmentally conscious	*Australians, Finns, French, British, Italians, Japanese, Koreans, Mexicans, Dutch, Polish, Hungarian, US-American*
complex garbage recycling (separation of various materials)	*Australians, Belgians, Brazilians, British, Chinese, French, Koreans, Dutch, Spanish, South Africans, Taiwanese*

A few true stories as an introduction:

There are many parking places in front of a Spaniard's apartment building in Germany. The parking spaces are not reserved and anyone can park there. There are no signs anywhere indicating who can park where. There is one parking place allowed per tenant. One day a neighbour of the Spaniard parks his car in the space that the Spaniard usually uses, just as the Spaniard is driving up. As soon as he arrives the neighbour comes running over to him saying, "Stop, stop, I'll move my car for you." The Spaniard is confused. He, too, could just as well park his car somewhere else, especially since there are more than enough empty spaces. Why is his neighbour so disturbed that he has parked his car in the "wrong" parking space?

An American student works in a German cafeteria. It annoys her that she is always expected to do an absolutely perfect job. For example, if she washes the floor with insufficient water, someone will point this out, saying it will never get clean that way. If she uses too much water, she will be told to make sure she dries it thoroughly! Once, after tying up the trash bag, she was made to untie it and fasten it with a special clasp to prevent it coming open. Another time when it was very hot she was reprimanded because she took off her white apron whilst washing the dishes. "You aren't allowed to work without an apron on!" Despite all this her co-workers are all in all very nice to her. However, she finds this perfectionism and constant nit- picking very nerve- wracking and in the end incomprehensible, especially since a cafeteria is not exactly a gourmet restaurant.

An English engineer working in Germany has rented a house and occasionally works in his garden. One day in Autumn, right when the leaves are turning and beginning to fall, he is busy pruning his roses when his neighbour mentions that it would be nice if he would rake up his leaves because they make a very untidy impression in the neighbourhood. The Englishman thinks this is a bit excessive but he wants to stay on good terms with his neighbour. So the next weekend, on Sunday, when he feels it would be nice to be out in the fresh air he decides to go out and rake up his leaves. He puts on his work clothes and sets to work when his neighbour comes out on the terrace with some guests. The Englishman waves to his neighbour, greeting him in a friendly manner. His neighbour, however, comes over to the garden wall and says, "But why do you have to do that work on a Sunday? That's not done in Germany. You should do it during the week." This whole situation is too much for the Englishman. Why would his neighbour, who is normally so nice and helpful, interfere and meddle so much in his personal affairs?

A Spanish couple who have recently moved to Germany are surprised to have many bins for different kinds of rubbish. Both of them find the system a bit difficult, but a nice neighbour explains the system to the woman several times.

When the biodegradable rubbish bin collection is introduced, the Spanish woman is invited over to her German neighbour's apartment. Her neighbour has placed different kinds of rubbish on her table, among them food-stuffs, old fruit and vegetables. She takes one piece of rubbish after another and explains whether they can go into the bio-bin or not. When she is finished she asks, "Do you understand this now?" The Spanish woman is partly amused, but also annoyed and a little offended. The German neighbour doesn't pick up on this reaction, and continues to give friendly tips on how to sort rubbish properly. The whole situation becomes too much for the Spanish couple, especially because much packaging carries no advice about which bin it belongs in. It finally gets to the point that one day when the Spanish woman is flying home for a holiday, she packs two suitcases full of the rubbish she didn't know how to dispose of in Germany and takes it home with her to Barcelona.

Definition of "Appreciation for Rules, Regulations and Structures"

In Germany there are more rules, regulations, ordinances, laws and formalities than anyone can count. Of course other countries also have social rules and laws, but in Germany their sheer number, the strict adherence to them and the rigidity of the reprimands and punishments set it apart from other countries. There are also many implied rules (for example, the expectation that people are always on time), rules that are limited to a very specific group (for example, apartment house rules), decrees that help to order public life (from rubbish disposal to traffic), norms used in the business world (like instructions, standardised procedures and regulations), systems and classification and systemic organisation of intellectual materials and so on. I use the word "structures" to cover all of the rules and regulations I have mentioned as well as all the others that may exist. Structures exist in every facet of life and are very rarely questioned. It is taken for granted that everyone will follow these structures and that anyone who doesn't will be reprimanded, even by strangers.

This culture standard is viewed as the most typical by foreigners who have come to Germany to work, and find themselves dealing with miles of red tape. Instead of being warmly welcomed, they are confronted with a mountain of bureaucratic procedures and papers: civic registration forms, opening a bank account, getting a driver's licence, applying for health insurance, and paying radio and television fees to list a few; all of which must be perfectly filled out, usually without any help. Landlords, neighbours, and others are often very keen on making sure that everyone observes and follows the laws and rules (house rules, cleaning days, quiet times on Sundays and over noon, areas where driving, parking or trespassing is not allowed). Often it is only when a foreigner has disobeyed one of the many rules that a German makes contact with them to point out the errors and to tell them which rule they have broken. Unfortunately these contacts often take the form of a lecture, a way of steering the foreigner firmly in the right direction.

Rules and Regulations as Helpful Institutions

Germans love structures such as rules and regulations. This is because they wish to have a clear and dependable understanding of what is expected; they want to have control over a situation, to be able to minimise the risks involved, and to prevent anything which could cause problems or mistakes. In short, they wish to achieve an *optimum end result*. Planning, or in other words creating a structure or system that functions as it is supposed to function, seems to be the key to mastering the tasks at hand. When Germans plan, organise, structure and systemise something, they do not do it for fun, but rather because they are convinced that the tasks at hand and common activities can best be managed in this way. For this reason quality managers work with exact instructions and software developers work with patterns or systems.

In social life this means that everything that has to do with relationships between people is controlled and steered as clearly and comprehensibly as possible, so that the German ideal of everyone being treated equally is possible. Formal and informal social interactions are often *so* explicitly arranged that everyone involved can clearly see which rights and duties they have.

Germans often use contracts as a way of organising and regulating their formal and business dealings with one another. The purpose of a contract is to provide security for all by ensuring that the issues are clear and that activities are kept running on track. The contents of such contracts are legally binding for both sides in Germany. The articles of a contract form the basis on which one can appeal, should some unforeseen event occur. For this reason, a great deal of care is taken to ensure that all possible sources of trouble in the relationship have been anticipated before a contract is signed.

A Chinese manager from a computer company is dealing with a German customer regarding the purchase and delivery of computer parts. The customer, after considerable deliberation, decides on a particular product. On the prearranged delivery date, the Chinese manager tells his customer that some minor changes have been unavoidable because of supply problems. He assures his customer that the product he has delivered is just as good and does exactly the same job as the one originally ordered, but the housing is slightly different. The German customer is not willing to accept the product because of these minor differences. The Chinese manager cannot understand the inflexibility of the customer.

When Germans strive for the optimum in their business dealings, they expect to be able to reach this level of perfection with the help of structures. When their goal is high quality (of products or in logistics, for example) they want to take the most effective, smoothest path to achieving this goal. For them the solution is to have structures, systems and norms that virtually eliminate any ambiguities and uncertainties and prevent problems.

Clear statements about competencies and responsibilities is one of the ways quality is ensured. The German system of vocational training is very specialised and plays a large part in guaranteeing competencies. Every job in the work force has explicit responsibilities which are respected. People do the job they are trained to do and assume the responsibilities appropriate to their level in the hierarchy. If problems arise for someone on the job because of a problem with the norms, regulations or structures, then the "guilt" belongs to whoever devised the framework and not the employee.

An Englishman works in Germany on an aluminium assembly line. He and a colleague are sent to a construction site to install an electrically operated door. After installing the door, the German is ready to leave, but the Englishman says that the door still needs to be wired up, otherwise it will not work. The German is surprised by this statement and says that this is the electrician's job. The Englishman is very puzzled by this remark, and by the German's unwillingness to even give it a try. Why would he refuse to finish the job?

An Englishman is the quality control manager of a German company. Due to a sudden increase in faulty products, he carries out an analysis of the problem and discovers that the same part is always to blame. The English manager approaches the worker responsible for this part to discuss the problem. The first reaction of the worker is to take out his blueprints to show the quality manager the specifications he has been given, after which he begins to check and measure the parts that are supposedly defective. He then explains in a very self-assured manner that the tolerance allowed is plus or minus 0.3 mm and, as the manager can see for himself, none of the parts he has produced exceed this. Therefore, he doesn't feel at all responsible for the problem. The English manager can't understand this reaction. He really doesn't care what the worker's excuse is, the parts don't work! How can he come up with such arguments! Blueprints or not, the worker's job is to make a functional part and he has failed.

In contrast to the scepticism other cultures feel about rigid structures, Germans regard norms and systems in the workplace as structures which are "tried and true": they worked well in the past and should therefore be kept. Norms are not something that have no meaning or something that someone has arbitrarily thought up: rather they are the result of all the efforts and expertise of people who have worked on similar problems in the past. If a current procedure or structure has proven itself to be the most effective way of doing something, Germans are keen to keep using it in the future.

This approach is taken not only in production but also management and administration, and jobs based on routines and repetition. If people want to criticise the current way of doing things, they are free to make suggestions for improvements and further developments. Only in exceptional situations, and then only with conclusive arguments, will the criticisms or suggestions of an individual be seen as carrying more weight than the accumulated wisdom of the many experts who have gone before.

The complete computer system in a Czech subsidiary of a German company must be replaced because it does not meet the necessary requirements. The Czech employees have analysed the problems and have made a decision about what they want to buy. Their preferred solution, however, overruns the budget that the German company has allotted. The Germans have to make a decision. The Czechs explain their analysis and the grounds for their solution. The Germans listen to them but then say, "Okay, but we have to start all over again." The Czechs are extremely frustrated that their hard work is not being taken seriously. The Germans from headquarters explain that there is already a company wide-strategy to solve this particular problem. The Czech subsidiary can expect financial aid as well as help with the implementation. Soon afterwards a group of German computer experts arrives to start work with their Czech colleagues on creating a perfect solution that will fulfill both the German company standards and the needs of the Czech operation. The solution they come up with is compared to the systems in place in other subsidiaries similar to the Czech subsidiary and the promised financial support is promptly provided. In the end, the Czechs are content with everything they have received. The solution is truly excellent and the Germans have kept their word in all respects. However the way the Germans dealt with the whole situation still seems very odd and time-consuming to the Czechs.

Germans always see a reason behind every structure, system and norm. Rules and regulations often have the same meaning for them as a proven method of solving, say, a mathematical problem. In production situations the norms take on a sort of symbolism for the world-famous German quality, or for progress in the sense of continual improvement.

Germans' Love of Organization

When Germans are working towards a goal, they reduce problems and disruptions along the way by planning and organising as actively (not reactively) as possible. For this reason, they set up all kinds of systems to help make their plans and intentions as tangible and feasible as possible: companies standardise the flow of work, procedures and processes; they define the responsibilities and competencies of each worker, as well as how work is to be shared; the flow of information is formalised and methods of dealing with problems are clearly laid out.

Work which is completely thought out and planned for the long-term is the ideal. Improvisation is used as an emergency measure to compensate for poor planning or unseen difficulties. It is seen as a sign of intelligence to get deeply involved in a task and to develop a systematic approach and strategy for implementation.

Germans dislike taking risks and go to great lengths to avoid things happening by accident. By planning, preparing and thinking through a job as well as possible, they try to eliminate all foreseeable difficulties and risks. Germans even have a saying for this: "It's better to be careful in advance, than to be smarter afterwards." They want to avoid changing their plans due to unforeseen circumstances. They attempt to find and eliminate all potential sources of mistakes, stumbling blocks and situations which could become dangerous.

Germans prefer using formal systems, preferably with written records such as time-sheets and performance reports to make clear and monitor who is responsible for what, and what has been agreed. For this reason, all jobs are burdened with a considerable amount of bureaucracy and formalities.

All of this effort pays off. Because people are forced to plan everything as optimally as possible right down to the last detail, it is possible to find the source of problems in order to make things run as smoothly as possible.

A French software engineer is working in Germany. Whilst working he runs across a problem for which he is able to find a solution. The solution, however, is not listed as one of the approved methods in the system instruction manual. When he asks his German boss if he could use his (not perfect, but functional) solution, the German says that this is not possible because it is not listed in the manual. He adds, however, that he will look into the matter. As expected, the boss doesn't find a solution in the manual that is equivalent to the French engineer's suggestion, so he says, "You can't do this because it's not in the manual and it could cause problems." As a compromise, the French engineer and his German boss write a new paragraph to add to the manual for every potential solution, thus documenting clearly what is allowed to be done and what is not. Both of them are happy with this.

Because of their desire to avoid risks, decision-making with Germans can often be quite a long, drawn-out process. They like to be as sure as possible that they have thought about and planned for as many eventualities as possible. They want to have a good overview of a situation, and would rather check something twice than make assumptions.

A great deal of important, normal work-related information is conveyed through very formal channels, like meetings, discussions, minutes, electronic mails, memos and other information distribution systems. In this way the information remains accessible and retrievable for all involved.

Job responsibilities are assigned by a department: not everyone does everything; instead who does what is clearly defined. People rarely take on tasks outside their job description, but will instead refer to the colleague responsible. People almost always go through the official and appropriate channels. Only the person who is responsible according to the organigram will be referred to, and no-one in a position of responsibility will be passed over. Responsibility is the key word that defines the scope of German business.

A French management expert is working in a local German chamber of commerce where companies can request and retrieve information and documents. The first question that her German secretary always asks when someone calls is where they are calling from. If the caller is calling from somewhere outside that chamber of commerce's jurisdiction then the secretary refers them immediately to the office responsible for that area and refuses to answer any questions, even if the caller only needs some simple or general information that would create little or no additional work load on her part.

In Germany, "responsibilities" is the key word in getting things done, and it also sets the boundary for what can be expected of colleagues and bosses. It is used to explain who normally does what, who is an expert in which field and who should be asked for help.

This is the German way of keeping people within their area of expertise, and the over-stepping of this boundary has to have a good reason, which must be explained to all concerned.

When Germans offer information about who is responsible for something, it is therefore intended as a genuine offer of help, not a way of avoiding getting involved.

A Czech woman is working as an assistant to the German boss of a bank in Prague. In the accounting procedures, the budget code and totals have to be entered on a special form. It is her job to fill out this form and then give it to her boss to sign. Once, when she is not at her desk, the German boss leaves a note written in large letters, saying, "Please enter the budget-code and totals and send the paperwork to the financial department. Thank you." She finds this rather amusing because if he had just filled it out himself he would have needed less time than he took to write her this note. But he would never do that. One of her other jobs is to sort through and deal with all of the seminars and courses that they are offered every day. She immediately throws out all of the offers that are completely irrelevant because they are either too expensive or not offered in Prague. After she has gone through them she gives them to her boss to look at. Once, after a day's absence, she finds a huge pile of offers on her desk. Each offer has a note from her boss attached to it with the following written on it: "Please check this out and get back to me to discuss it." As usual she throws most of them away and discusses only the few remaining offers with her boss.

It is quite possible that many Germans think that their non-German colleagues do not respect the "rules" of responsibility as they should.

The Germans over-compensate by adhering to their prescribed areas of competence and responsibility even more rigidly than before.

Germans are easily annoyed when something does not work because of a lack of organisation or because of disruptions. In such cases they are more likely to look for the person responsible than they are to look for a solution.

Most power struggles and conflicts between Germans have to do with responsibility. Managers are seen as representatives of the organisational structures, and for this reason most employees are very diligent about showing their respect to them with regards to following these rules, regulations and structures.

Attention to Detail

Germans are perfectionists and have very high expectations when it comes to even the smallest details. Because of their perfectionism they break down ideas into the smallest possible components. Details are not of secondary importance and are therefore given a great deal of attention. Germans believe that the true value and quality of something is directly related to the workmanship and quality of the details. Most problems are thus traced back to the details. There is a saying in German, "The devil is in details."

For this reason, it is characteristic that Germans
- make exact and detailed plans,
- minimize possible sources of errors beforehand,
- are well prepared for meetings and negotiations (for example by bringing transparencies for the overhead projector and handouts),
- highly value neatness and orderliness (for example, through filing systems, stock-keeping and warehousing).

Germans aspire to accuracy, perfection, precision, and 100% mistake-free production in industry. Their goal is a perfect product. Production guidelines are strictly adhered to, and it is ensured that the work actually takes place according to the specified norms. Proof of a good job is customer satisfaction, and the customers of German companies expect quality products which are error-free. A company's image and future success are dependent upon this. Perfection is discernible in the way unimportant details are not forgotten, but attended to. In order to reach these goals of perfection, it is important not to make approximations but to follow the guidelines and norms exactly!

An English manager working for a German auto-parts manufacturing plant is responsible for the final production stages of their new axle and the packaging and shipping of the finished product. Since the development of the axle has taken longer than planned, his timeline has been shortened. In order to meet his deadline the Englishman has worked over-time every day for two weeks. In the end, the company is able to meet the deadline, which makes the Englishman happy, since it is a key order. He is convinced that his German boss will also be pleased with the outcome, so he is very surprised when he is summoned into his boss's office to be told that there is a mistake in the diagram of the axle which is in the brochure for the automobile manufacturer. The Englishman has not used, as required, their customer's standard typeface, and would he please correct it.

The desire for perfection on the part of some Germans can often limit their ability to be spontaneous and flexible.

A Spaniard is continually amused by his German colleague. They are jointly responsible for the specialised computer programme used in manufacturing. A few minutes ago they received a phone call to let them know that a delegation from another plant will arrive in an hour, and that they would appreciate a presentation about the software. Management wants the two computer specialists to put something together for their guests which will explain the software and the reasons why it has really improved production. This is to take place at 10:00 a. m., in room 20. The German specialist is clearly in shock and stutters, "I'm sorry, but I can't do it at such short notice." For a while everyone tries to convince him that with all of his expertise he could easily talk from his own experiences. In the end the Spaniard gives the presentation – not in perfect German – but he is the one who feels confident that he will be able to explain the essentials to their guests.

Issues to do with lending and borrowing money are always resolved down to the very last cent, even in everyday situations between colleagues. This is an example of German exactness and fairness. To "pay the German way" (or "Deutsch zahlen") means that everyone pays separately for exactly what they have ordered.

A group of colleagues including Germans and Czechs goes out to lunch together in a restaurant in Pilsen. The German team leader pays the bill from a special fund for business-related meals. The bill is for 156 Crowns. He pays the exact amount and leaves four crowns on the table. The Germans are still calculating how much four Crowns is in Euros when a Czech colleague says, "Only four Crowns?" This starts a discussion. "Is that too little? How much do Czechs usually leave?" The German feels under attack. Now he really wants to know exactly how much one pays for a normal tip in the Czech Republic. Explaining "normal" or "proper" tipping behaviour is difficult for the Czech because one tips according to the situation and depending upon how satisfied one is. This explanation is of no use to the German. He doesn't give up! What is the standard tip? How should he tip in the future? His Czech colleague is totally embarrassed.

Ambivalence

Germans are well aware of their love of rules but they are singularly ambivalent about their own behaviour. They see the reasoning behind their adherence to such structures, but they themselves often suffer personally from the consequences of such inflexibility. Many Germans actually see it as a sign of social progress to be able to disregard various rules, and enjoy quoting studies which show, for example, that only a minority of the population drive within the official speed limits, that many of the social rules regarding etiquette are no longer valid, or that many companies would have to shut down if they actually followed all of the rules and regulations, and so on. These subtle social changes are probably not obvious to non-Germans, especially if they have not lived in Germany for very long. They see Germans as they are here and now and certainly do not have the impression that they take their rules and regulations lightly.

Let me bring this phenomenon into perspective with a few of my own observations. Every person, every social group and every generation, follows the rules and regulations which they consider important and which help them to organise central aspects of their lives. However, the same persons or groups often overlook and ignore other rules and regulations which they see as being useless and old-fashioned. Every German can list a large number of examples in which he or she has been casual about, and others, in which they wouldn't survive without at least a bare minimum (as defined by Germans) of order and regulation. This can be illustrated by a real-life example:

During an intercultural training session I conducted about Germany, a group of English people greatly amused the rest of the members with a role-play that they called "Recycling the tea bag." The teabag with its contents ended up in the biodegradable bin, the metal staple ended up in the metal recycling bin, the string went in with the normal rubbish, and the paper label ended up in the paper bin. I felt that this was a caricature of the German character. Still laughing about it, I shared this story with my next class, a group of German business students, during a rather heated discussion about whether the German obsession with rules really exists. What followed was complete and stony silence, until one student, who was obviously embarrassed, said, "But we really do do it that way."

In this example, it is not the tea bag but the rubbish recycling which exemplifies the modern German love of structures and rules, which in this case are being followed because of the desire to protect the environment. Keeping to the "good old" tradition of making rules and regulations and sticking to them serves this social goal well.

Here is another example: large companies undeniably suffer from the fact that communication is formalised and regulated. Without the informal channels along which information is quickly dispersed, there would be great problems. What can be done to support informal channels of communication? One possibility is a trainee *programme*, which could, in the future, help to strengthen such informal structures.

One evening an American went out with some of his German friends to a wine bar. Since he didn't want to drink alcohol he ordered himself a Spezi (a mixture of Cola and Fanta). When the waiter said that they didn't have Spezi, the American ordered a Cola. Later in the evening a friend of his ordered a Fanta. The American was annoyed. If they had Cola and Fanta, why couldn't they have mixed him a Spezi?

This sort of thing annoys Germans as well and it happens every day. These people are following the rules to the last degree.

To bring things into perspective, there are areas of German life which are highly organised for good reason, and in which "what is said really goes." There are, however, other areas which are completely disorganised, and in these cases visitors to Germany miss that famous "German perfectionism." The meagre state of childcare for working families is an example of this gap in organisation. A good example of disorganisation in the workplace is the lack of good training and integration programmes for non-Germans. As a result, these colleagues feel unwanted and in the way, pushed around ineffectively from one department or position to another. In such situations the

81

result is doubly disappointing. Germans fight fiercely against their own image, but at the same time can only compensate for missing structures or faults in the system through improvisation, which is inadequate.

The Pros and Cons of the Appreciation for Rules, Regulations and Structures

The advantage of the culture standard *"Appreciation for Rules, Regulations and Structures"* is clearly that a well-established system makes excellent results possible.

The disadvantages are as follows:
- Once a plan has been made, Germans become single-minded about putting it into practice. If an unforeseen event occurs or there is something standing in their way, they are often thrown off balance and become confused about how they should continue. It is not uncommon for some to lose their composure or even panic.
- In large companies, systems and structures can become so bureaucratic that cooperation can become hindered. There are so many regulations, formalities and defined areas of competence and responsibility to keep in mind, all requiring some sort of documentation or approval, that doing business becomes slow and difficult. Under these circumstances even things that by and large make sense start to look questionable.

A Frenchman working in Germany has just received a phone call from France. He is asked if a long-awaited decision has been made yet. The French have been calling about this issue for two weeks and he, as always, has to put them off. The head of division, head of department and a specialist, all of whom are located in Germany, have a say in the final decision. One of them is on holiday and the other two are away on business, so the decision that is so important to the French must be further delayed. The good news is that next week a meeting is planned and the Frenchman will finally be able to call his colleagues in France with an answer to their question. Until then the Germans are "thinking about it."

- In Germany, it can be difficult to get an overview of a project because of the high degree of specialisation and the many different people and positions involved. The problems that occur during the project nevertheless have to be addressed spontaneously, and the value of the systemised and structured approach is lost.

– Another negative aspect of the German obsession with organisation down to the smallest detail is that once a goal or a structure has been planned, it is followed through, even though it may not suit changing conditions. It is very hard to change course midway through. Those responsible for getting a job done are often so fixated on their plans, deadlines, agreements, and how they can avoid mistakes that they completely lose track of the big picture. The system becomes inflexible and unresponsive.

– Germans use structures not only to organise their work effectively but also to establish boundaries and privileges, such as personal space and private life. When it is break-time it really *is* break-time; when it is time to go home, it really *is* time to go home; and when an employee is on holiday, they are usually not to be contacted. There is also the possibility that sloppy workmanship and laziness are be blamed on "just following the rules" or "only doing the job."

It is not only Americans who find it rude when no-one answers the telephone during the morning tea and coffee break or when the person being called is on holiday, at a meeting or is just not at their desk.

An Englishman is the quality control manager for a German industrial supply company. Because a delivery deadline is getting tight he would like his employees to take their lunch break later. The German employees say this is not possible because lunch is from 12 to 1 p. m., and not later. The English manager is quite annoyed: why are the Germans so inflexible?

– Behind such obedience to rules often lies nothing less than fear and uncertainty. In order to avoid risks, people follow rules and regulations as exactly as possible, with the idea that "It's better to be safe than sorry."

– In everyday life as well as in the workplace, the tendency to fall back on what is legally stipulated, regulated and clearly spelt out costs time and makes it difficult to come up with creative solutions to conflicts. Sometimes rules are shamelessly interpreted and used to give a personal advantage.

A Brazilian living in Germany has just returned from a visit to Brazil. He is suffering from jet lag and is completely exhausted. His German neighbour, who is renovating his apartment right next door, makes matters worse by hammering and drilling so loudly that he can't sleep. He gets out of bed and goes next door to explain his problem to his neighbour and to ask him to stop. The neighbour answers, "I have the right to work until 10 p. m., then I will stop."

– When someone adamantly sticks to their rights, a plan or a business procedure which is clearly defined by rules and regulations, they may not seem polite and objective, but rather rude and authoritarian.

A German comes running out of the production department into the logistics department and screams at his Hungarian colleague, "We are running out of pumps! We need 500 'A' pumps immediately, otherwise we will have to stop production. See to it that you deal with this problem!" When the Hungarian calls the suppliers, they say they can't deliver the pumps before next week. A little while later the German comes roaring in again. Of course he is not happy with the answer. He wants his colleague to call the supplier again. "We need those pumps tomorrow. Don't forget that the suppliers have a contract with us and we are an important company! Put pressure on them!" The Hungarian calls again. The supplier then says that if it's so important, he could wangle a deal so that he could deliver 500 pumps by Friday. The German, who is standing behind the Hungarian, hears the word "Friday" and grabs the phone. "What do you mean you can't deliver tomorrow! You have a contract with us! You will deliver tomorrow! Otherwise our production line will have to be stopped and that will be very expensive for you – I hope you have good insurance! I expect this delivery to be confirmed by fax, today! I would also like to point out to you that you will see the repercussions of this when it's time for supplier evaluations." He then hangs up. The Hungarian colleague, who by this time is as white as a ghost, is then told, "You have to be tougher with our suppliers. That's the only way you'll get what you want, as you just saw for yourself. Don't forget that you represent the company, and the supplier has a contract with us." With that, the German walks out.

– Germans are convinced that their systems will, without a doubt, result in success. Some are so confident of their expertise that they fail to notice that they appear completely arrogant: they never question their own system or way of looking at the world.

Recommendations

Suggestions for non-Germans Working with Germans
- Don't think that Germans are directing their obsession with rules and norms against you personally, or trying to be patronising. They are just being "professional," as they see it. Be comforted by the fact that Germans act the same way towards each other as well.
- Try to understand the social aspects of structures, norms, rules and regulations.This will help you see that behaviour which may seem hard or stubborn also has a very human side to it: Germans like life to be clear, understandable, fair, honest and organised.

Suggestions for Germans Working with non-Germans
- Don't expect that your wishes, problems, expectations or demands will be immediately and clearly evident to others. Instead, it is likely that people from cultures with a more relaxed attitude towards structures will *not* automatically understand you.
- Explain your "structure" to them! Tell them the reasons, the context and the goals and explain to them *why* you would like or need something done in your special, German-structured way. Only by doing this will your wishes have a chance of being understood and carried out; otherwise they will be seen as pure authoritarianism.
- If you are able to explain clearly when and why structures can and can't be changed, others will find it easier to follow those rules and regulations which really *are* important, because they will not be seen as examples of pig-headedness or authoritarianism.
- Create new structures in cooperation with your international colleagues when you start to work on a new project, rather than just using existing ones. Your colleagues undoubtedly understand their situation and conditions better than you do and vice versa. Only in this way can you develop a structure that will fulfil the needs of both you and your colleagues.

Historical Background

The entire Western world places great importance on "legal morality," the foundation of which already existed in ancient times. An approach corresponding to the so-called "social contract model" had already evolved in the Greek city-states, which implied commitment to an *abstract* society (the state) and not to a clan or a group of known or related people generally called a "community" (Kindermann). Social life was governed by laws, and prominent Greek philosophers such as Socrates, Aristotle and Plato endeavoured to find unquestionable ethical and judicial standards against which the validity of such laws could be measured. Later on, the concepts of equality and reason also formed the basis for Roman law. Roman citizenship was not based on membership of a community (like nationality or ethnic origin) but was offered to subjects who were prepared to co-operate with the Roman state. Legal argument was well-developed in Rome. The Romans governed on the basis of clearly defined laws, and not through the people who laid down the principles of the laws (Hofstede 1993). This tradition was subsequently adopted by the emerging church and later, by European states.

Along with Christianity, these concepts and principles were introduced to the area now known as Germany, and Roman law became the basis of modern continental European legislation. The question is, how could these general developments have exerted such an impact on Germany as to make the cultural standard *"Appreciation for Rules, Regulations and Structures"* so conspicuous?

The forerunners of German principalities and minor states were not city-states as in ancient Greece, but relatively manageable tribal communities. They too had developed rules – homogeneous rituals and ways of doing things – which on the one hand furthered cohesion in the community and on the other hand made survival possible. As violation of these rules meant exclusion from the community and total ruin for the individual, it was strongly avoided (Molz 1994). In this way, the foundation was laid in what is now Germany for a readiness to create and accept rules. This foundation was partially retained in the small states that followed and was increasingly bound to Christian norms during the middle ages, eventually gaining universal acceptance (see the chapter on *"Rule-Oriented, Internalised Control"*).

Life during the time of the German *small states* also gave their members the chance to learn something else: precision of thought (Gehlen 1975). This resulted from the fact that broad intellectual and moral experiences characteristic of extensive communities and differentiated systems of rule were not possible. This was true even for

Prussia, which was an artificial state, and for the Habsburg Empire, of which only a small part was German-speaking. The people became accustomed to living within restricted conditions in a boundaried society and therefore took pride in "depth" not "breadth." The diligence of the craftsman and precision of the "Meistersinger" were recognised as the highest virtues: reliability and order earned similarly high praise. In the longer term this laid the foundation for the current German orientation toward quality, which has been passed down by way of rules.

There is a connection between the nature of structures which are characterised by the joy of systems, order and the positive results this brings, with the way the Enlightenment reached the German states (Kielinger 1996). In Germany, the ideas of the Enlightenment arrived long before actual political changes occurred. The negative results of the system of small states were obvious, and educated members of the middle-class yearned for a stable and progressive order. The philosophies of political emancipation (small-state absolutism still prevailed) and the Enlightenment were still far apart. In the chasm between these two philosophies came the abstract idea of a centralised, regulating state, which reconciled the ruling classes with the middle and lower classes. The state was increasingly idealised as a "higher moral principle" (Münch 1993) which balanced conflicting interests and integrated them into a systematic and universal legal system. In the 19th century the state as an entity achieved the long-desired orderly structure, in contrast with the reactionary nature of social relationships at that time. "During the formation of the modern German, state, the characteristic 'state-burdened', bureaucratic thinking developed, which is in no other Western country as deeply ingrained in the mentality of a people as it is in Germany." (Althaus et al. 1992c, p. 94; see also Nipperdey 1991).

At the same time (and paradoxically), certain individual states, especially those under Napoleonic influence, were also satisfying this need. The Napoleonic "land reallocation" reform of 1806 brought concepts of enlightened government and standardisation to heterogeneous, often tiny territories with very different political and social traditions and lifestyles. "Standardisation and nationalisation through reform legislated and organised from the top down means that the concepts of central economic control and the organs of state administration must be created" (Althaus et al. 1992c, p. 94). Laws and regulations which exerted tight control over the everyday life of citizens were enacted, including such diverse areas as time management, hygiene, work houses for the poor and homeless, the location of manure heaps, appropriate dress and pre-marital sexual relations. These developments brought obvious modernisation and progress, including the end of serfdom, the foundation of a constitutional state, freedom of religious belief, the right to legal redress, social security and progress in medical treatment. Both of the results of nationalisation – the welcome reforms as well as the absolute state control – left particularly deep traces in German life even though they occurred all over Europe; because they could manifest themselves more drastically and unavoidably in the territorial confines of the German small states (Althaus et al. 1992c). It remains a moot point whether the ruling classes modernised as a result of their enlightened insights or whether they were motivated by a desire to retain power (Kalberg 1988). Whatever the case, the end result was due to the relative success of the "state" in generating respect and even worship: in our context the "structure."

At the same time another development took place: since German nobility did not open up to embrace the economically strengthening middle-class, the latter defiantly developed its own values and norms of behaviour in the 18th and 19th century, which were supposedly based on the natural and inherent values of the German person. They were seen as being opposed to the artificiality and formality of the French-inspired nobility. Accordingly, the social rituals of cleanliness came to signify inner "cleanliness": the maxim "cleanliness is next to Godliness" had significance in Germany. A healthy (because clean) body was the home of a healthy (therefore clean) intellect. The equating of exterior cleanliness and order with inner worth "is found throughout Germany" (Wagner 1996, p. 51). This view can be applied to all contexts in which *order* is possible and also reinforces everything I have described so far under the culture standard *"Appreciation for Rules, Regulations and Structures."*

Security and order were constantly under threat in the area which is now Germany. Most generations experienced prolonged *existential upheavals.* "In the course of its history Germany has endured so many periods of turmoil and chaos, that it has learnt to appreciate the blessings of order," writes Gorski (1996, p. 91). "There are clever people who suspect that the root of German perfectionism, German desire for order, German obsession with security lies in the Thirty-Year-War ... For thirty years, at that time nearly one and a half generations, anarchy, arbitrary use of power, lawlessness reigned in Germany." (Gorski 1996, p. 92). Germany was powerless and became the almost completely devastated battlefield of other nations. As a territorially fragmented country at the centre of Europe, Germany had previously, and for centuries to come, been besieged within its own borders and often threatened by total disintegration and destruction. The Holy Roman Empire, dating back to Charles the Great and tracing its claim to Rome, experienced serious weaknesses after the late Middle Ages (Gross 1971), the most prominent of which was the lack of an integral concept of state and a chronic weakness of central authority. Thus, Germany had increasingly become a fictitious structure that was no match for the demands of practical politics. With the Westphalian Peace of 1648, the influence of the church as structuring entity had also decreased significantly. Germany disintegrated into a multitude of small and minute states – when Napoleon's "land reallocation" reform began there were over 1000 state-like structures. Generations were stricken and decimated by wars and epidemics, and as a result declined into provincialism and deep insecurity. The only hope of security lay with submission to the rule of the current petty prince (Gorski 1996).

Repeated *existential upheavals* have occurred in recent history as well: social dislocation in the industrialisation revolution, the crisis in the period of the foundation of modern Germany, the First World War, inflation and the world economic crisis in the 1920s, the Second World War and the ensuing division of Germany.

Each trauma intensified the yearning for stability and order and for strong authorities capable of avoiding such horrors in the future (Craig 1985). It strengthened the tendency towards an "esteem for structures" that had latently developed and been nurtured for centuries. The intensified desire of the German population for security explains the mind-set that the common good can only be preserved by strict observance of laws and regulations. "With such experiences in the collective memory, it is indeed no small wonder that the Germans nowadays would not leave anything to chance. Everything is planned in detail" (Gorski 1996, p. 93).

In summary: the Germans have a history of structures which surpasses that of other Western countries:

- The structures they developed in their "Holy Roman Empire of the German Nation" were extremely complex and committed to a lofty ideal: the Empire as protector of the church (Nipperdey 1991). Since this aim could initially and on the whole be realised, a positive attitude toward the state arose.
- From the late Middle Ages onward, the preservation of these structures became problematic (continual battles with the Pope) since the weakness of the central authority ultimately led to centuries of territorial division and political impotence on the grand stage of the great European powers (Nipperdey 1991). As the structures developed further, they hindered national development and were ultimately the reason for many catastrophes.
- Parallel to this, there was (1) great yearning for "intact" structures that would make life easier – perhaps because the old structures had proven to be such a hindrance, and also (2) real successes, which could in turn be attributed fundamentally to strong structures (Nipperdey 1991), such as the medieval Imperial Diets, the development and significance of cities as legal institutions, the monasteries, the reforms of the Enlightenment, industrialisation (effective development in the 19th century up to the contribution of the DIN norms to the economical miracle), the German unification of 1871 (bureaucracy and the military proved to be success factors) or also the establishment of the Federal Republic of Germany in 1949.

A certain fixation on structures, both in reality and in wishful thinking, as well as the ongoing practice of designing, constructing, altering and refining structures therefore have plausible explanations.

. . . rules, regulations

Rule-Oriented, Internalised Control

How Germans are perceived by other cultures	
children are self-reliant	*Australians, Brazilians, Mexicans*
not very relaxed or easy-going, don't laugh very much, quite serious, exaggerate problems	*Australians, Brazilians, British, Chinese, Finns, French, Dutch, US-Americans*
thorough, detail-oriented, (too) precise, work hard and with stamina/perseverance, mistakes are not allowed and when they occur Germans notice them	*British, Chinese, Finns, French, Malaysians, Poles, Spanish, South Africans, Czech, Hungarians*
conduct themselves in a disciplined, serious, strict, precise way when it comes to norms, rules, regulations and laws	*Chinese, French, Indians, Japanese, Mexicans, Dutch, Poles, Spanish, Czech, Hungarians, US-Americans*
both obedient and authoritarian	*French, Poles, Czech, Hungarians, US-Americans*
reliable and responsible and expect the same from everyone else	*Bulgarians, Chinese, French, Italians, Poles, Spanish, South Africans, Czechs, Hungarians*
quickly annoyed when plans change	*Indians, Japanese*
stubborn, opinionated, inflexible; often don't admit to having made a mistake and have difficulty saying they are sorry	*Chinese, Indians, Italians, Japanese, Swedes, Czechs, Hungarians*
have a strong sense of fairness	*Czechs*
self-critical, search for negative aspects of themselves, strong sense of guilt about the Second World War	*Finns*

An important consideration when comparing cultures is whether abstract, general and universal rules, laws and agreements are meant to be strictly followed or whether it is allowable to bend them to serve personal or social interests. In other words, where does the "ethical responsibility" or sense of duty lie: in rules that are relatively independent of individuals, relationships and situations, or in the people, who either put the rules to use or choose to ignore them depending on the situation?

The Definition of Rule-Oriented, Internalised Control

Germans are inclined to answer the above question with the first alternative: rules are binding. There are clear, universal guidelines which are valid for all humans regardless of any social or political connections an individual might have. In effect this leads to a society that, in contrast to Asian and East-Slavic cultures, uses many formal and informal rules and laws to define what is "good" or "bad." The German constitution, German social and cultural norms and the countless rules and procedures found in professional life as well as everyday situations are based on this understanding.

From the point of view of others, Germans "follow the rules" and generally identify themselves quite strongly with their jobs, taking their work, roles and tasks, as well as the associated responsibilities very seriously. They want to do what they do *well* and they concentrate hard on getting it done.

Once Germans start planning, organising, and structuring something, they do not do it for fun, but rather because they are convinced that the task at hand can best be managed this way. There is one condition needed for these structures to be put into action, and this is the essence of the culture standard *"Rule-Oriented, Internalised Control." One must be able to count on everyone involved.* Once something is planned and organised, everyone is expected to stay within the boundaries of their job description and do their job. The system only functions if everyone works together. Being rule-oriented and having internal control means following all of the rules, systems and structures that apply to a specific context, but also never losing sight of the more abstract and universal rules, general agreements and contracts which are independent of specific people and situations.

For Germans, following rules and respecting structures has a moral value and is equated with being reliable. In the workplace, an important function of a boss is to represent the structure.

A Korean once tried to describe how the culture standards *"The Appreciation for Rules and Regulations"* and *"Rule-Oriented, Internalised Control"* overlap. "Whoever manages a project can assume that his ideas will be put into action as soon as he has written his plan down on paper. In this way the information doesn't get lost and confirmation of acceptance is not necessary." He was very surprised at the ease with which new programmes were introduced, because the instructions for them were just carried out. Ideally, everyone gives their best and works hard on their part of a cooperative project to make sure that the common goal is achieved. By doing so, Germans seem to be able to motivate themselves with the intricacies of their own particular task.

An Indian is responsible for the coordination between an Indian software company and a German company. In his role he supervises both German and Indian employees. It never fails to amaze him how motivated the Germans are to work. When he delegates a new job, his German employees take pains to do their jobs well and they help each other when necessary. It is noticeable that it is important to them that the project gets done with as few problems as possible, although none of them will personally benefit from this. Organising a task well and then completing it seems to have intrinsic worth to Germans.

Reliability is not only achieved through external control exerted by authorities, but by people choosing to do what is expected of them. The non-German participants in my inter-cultural seminars are often quite amazed at some of the examples I have of this, such as German customs officers believing without question someone who says he has nothing to declare. It is also evident in the fact that very few people ride public transportation without buying a ticket, or that businesses often display their wares outside their doors unattended. Internalised control means that whole business areas in Germany run efficiently with only occasional supervision and checking. For this reason, responsibility is a quality often listed by non-Germans when describing Germans.

When Germans make a decision or agree upon a common goal, they can be depended on to carry it through without going back on their word or making changes. After entering an agreement, they do not have the feeling that *others* expect something from them; instead it is clear that they will do what they have agreed to do and that they themselves want to do it. During the process of planning, organising, negotiating, or even at the point of accepting a job, Germans are already identifying with the task. This is what is meant by "internalised control": accepting that some rules are "for the best" and that an action is "necessary" means that an individual is controlling themselves and there is no need for external checking-up. The consequence of such thinking is that norms and plans are followed. If an individual is completely convinced that decisions and rules are meaningful, respecting them and acting in accordance with them becomes part of their personality.

From the individual perspective, this type of self-control is seen as a form of personal autonomy and self- determination; seen from an outside perspective, it allows self-initiated and independent action. In Germany, this type of autonomy is widely expected and individuals are held responsible for the consequences of their actions. Consequently violations of rules or other "disturbing" actions will not normally lead, in the first instance, to conflict with a superior; but rather cause internal conflict and discontent with self.

The German director of a sales district has passed on documents from his Czech employees to middle management. Now he has discovered that the documents contain mistakes. At best, the German director should have examined all of the documents, however due to the large number of them this is generally impossible and only spot checks are carried out. He is angry about having been criticised by his superiors and reprimands his Czech employees for having given him such sub-standard documents. "Do you realise that you've made me look like an idiot!" he complains. However at the same time a colleague, who sits in the same office with the German boss, notices that he is just as angry with himself, "I should've checked this! Why didn't I do it right?" His Czech colleague doesn't understand him: Why is he taking this incident so much to heart? Why is he so involved on a personal level? It's not really that important, it's just a routine thing.

Since Germans internalise structures, norms, agreements and goals, they are very reliable when it comes to the *task* (see the culture standard *"Objectivism"*). Personal relationships have little effect on this conscientiousness. Regardless of whether or not the boss is "a nice guy" or the colleagues are comfortable working with each other, each employee has a job to fulfill and, generally this is exactly what they want to do. Germans believe in doing their job well, because it is part and parcel of occupying "that" position and having "those" tasks. First and foremost, a sense of duty is owed to the concrete guidelines and specifications of a task or job, together with loyalty to the company and reliability regarding contractual agreements.

At least in the professional sphere, duty comes before pleasure, and personal well-being is not a high priority. Whether someone wants to do something or not, or has a personal problem which is using up a great deal of energy, or has invested patience, or is having fun – these factors are not the decisive ones. It is the job of everyone who has agreed to a contract or who has taken on a job to do their duty, carry out their responsibilities and do the job as well as they can. In return they will, of course, be paid. Conscientiousness comes from being tough on one's self and having self-discipline.

A group of Czechs were at a trade fair with an employee from their German partner company, who was in charge of them during the fair. One evening they all got together for a drink and ended up having a stimulating conversation until 2 a. m., The next morning the Czechs arrived at their trade-fair stand at 9:30 a. m., instead of the usual 8:30. The German, who had been there since 8:00 a. m., demanded to know "Why are you so late? It's not OK for you to go out at night drinking and then neglect your work the next day!" The Czech employees were shocked. What's the problem? Why does it matter? The trade-fair only opened at 9:00 a.m and anyway, there were no visitors that early.

Germans find it alien that someone would expect to be praised for doing something that is their duty or part of their job. Just because someone does their normal work does not mean that they are being particularly helpful, pleasing or deserving of praise. It's just their job. A favour in Germany is something that goes over and above the normal line of duty. This is why Germans rarely give praise and why most things are taken for granted, unless something is specifically singled out as being exceptional. When there is any kind of positive feedback, it is more likely to be a thank-you than specific praise.

In summary, Germans find it necessary:
– to stick to their roles, responsibilities and competencies;
– to keep their promises, arrangements, agreements and contracts;
– to implement decisions;
– to follow guidelines exactly;
– to be reliable and punctual;
– to take responsibility for their actions.

If a person is able to fulfill all of these requirements, he or she will be seen as a reliable, correct, conscientious and valuable worker and a colleague who deserves to be trusted. The saying "Being German means doing something just for its own sake" is understandable in this context.

Consensus: the Best Basis for Rule-Oriented, Internalised Control

The *structure* that everyone follows is often the end result of a collective decision making process or an agreement between all involved people. Consensus is something that all Germans cherish and is considered to be the highest form of participation: everyone thinks about an issue together. They discuss the different aspects and then make a decision which is based on the input of all. The process as well as the outcome is often written down in the form of minutes. It can understandably take quite a while before a decision is made. However, the acceptance and commitment level among the participants is very high due to the fact that everyone has had the chance to share their concerns and reservations throughout the discussion and decision making process.

This approach to decision making is often the cause of conflicts when foreigners work with Germans. This is especially the case when Germans think they have come to a common decision with their foreign colleagues and later realise that they only *thought* there was consensus. For their partners it was never clear that an agreement had been made, or they do not consider the decision to be binding, as the Germans do.

A new computerised logistics system is being introduced to a company, first at the headquarters and then in the subsidiaries. The system is quite complicated, so a group of meetings has been set up for members of the German headquarters and the end-users of the system in Hungary. The Germans' intention is to introduce the system and to provide the Hungarians with an opportunity to voice any concerns or wishes they may have, so that any adjustments necessary from their side can be made before the system is put in place. The Hungarians are at the tenth and (supposedly) last meeting in Germany. Up until this point the Hungarians have agreed with the Germans and have made very few suggestions. The German logistics manager is a bit surprised by this, so just to be on the safe side he asks if the system in its current form will really work for the Hungarians, and if they can see themselves using it without problems. The Hungarians all say yes and the subject – from the planning side at least– seems to be finalised. Two days later the Germans receive a fax from the Hungarians in which they have listed so many problems that it could be read as a total rejection of the new system. The Germans fly into a fit of rage: what was the point of meeting together day after day if this is the end result!

Many other conflicts are stirred up when Germans try to achieve consensus with colleagues who have completely different opinions. Germans express opinions, discuss, protest against less than optimal solutions, try to come to a consensual decision and then follow it through. The French, for example, see Germans in such situations as being very stubborn:

A French company has taken over a German company. It's clear who has the power, but that doesn't stop the Germans from stating their opinions loud and clear, especially when they are different! The two opinions collide with one another dramatically when it comes to the technical developments. The Germans fight for their position in every meeting. The French management, as well as the French employees, all think that the Germans are absolutely pig-headed and unwilling to work cooperatively.

Germans are not very good at re-opening negotiations or seizing advantages which appear during the course of a project: finding new ways of doing something once a plan has been made does not come easily. They want to define the structure first, work out a timetable, and then work within these guidelines. Furthermore, if someone has a better idea about how to go about something, they must first discuss it with all of the people involved, including the boss, so that it can be jointly accepted as a "new rule" before it can actually go into effect. Germans do not see improvisation and acting on one's own authority as being constructive methods of working together, but rather as an act of egoism.

A Polish woman works for a German company in Poland. She and her Polish colleagues have worked together to improve various aspects of their work process. When the owner of the company notices that the processes have been changed, he asks the Polish woman why she and her colleagues have interfered with the process. "Because it's better this way," she answers, to which the German snaps that she shouldn't make any changes until she's discussed them with him. The Polish employee is outraged: it seems that she and her colleagues don't have the right to do or say anything! They should just follow orders! No-one expects them to have any ideas! Germans are so bossy!

Living the Conviction

Sometimes Germans identify themselves so strongly with a certain situation, the introduction of a principle or the responsibility for a system that they actually "live it." They slip into the role of being a moralistic role-model. The classic example of this German trait which is *always* mentioned in seminars regarding German behaviour is that of German pedestrians who wait at the red light, even when there is no car in sight. They justify this by saying that it is to educate children to be aware and careful on the streets. They are just being good examples for them.

Another aspect of the culture standard *"Rule-Oriented, Internalised Control"* is the already-discussed German trait of telling people about their mistakes, pointing out which rules they have just broken, and generally getting involved in other people's business. This intervention is based on the belief that a well-functioning system will eliminate sources of error and danger, and Germans want to help their system – their society – achieve this so it can run smoothly. I have already mentioned one example of this: environmental protection. Since progress can best be achieved (a) by a grass roots movement and (b) when everyone works together, some people even become fanatic recycling missionaries.

The German boss of a Czech employee can both praise her for a job well done and simultaneously find cause for criticism. When she fails to meet a deadline for entering certain data into the bank's computer system he gets very angry. He doesn't accept her excuse that the documentation that she needed had not been forwarded to her on time: "You should come earlier when you know you can't finish things on time! You should have informed me that you probably wouldn't complete this job on time and asked me what we could do about it!" He was really very angry.

Whilst driving in Germany an Englishman notices that several different cars which have driven behind him for quite a while on a winding road have blinked their lights at him. This seems like very aggressive behaviour to him. When he gets to his destination and has parked his car, his German friend points out to him that his brake lights appear to be broken. Then he remembers the flashing of headlights and his friend confirms his suspicion that his non-functioning brake lights could have been the reason for the German drivers' behaviour. It was meant as a warning sign!

When Germans assume the role of a "good example," they want to demonstrate to everyone that they are particularly precise, reliable, goal-oriented, punctual and willing to work. This can sometimes feel like they are showing-off because the main priority is to demonstrate how seriously the responsibility or duty is being taken, rather than anything else more central to the job. There are strong parallels between this behaviour and experiences that belong in the school or childhood, so it is no coincidence that scenes like the following can make one feel like a child again.

It is winter in Prague and it is snowing outside. When a Czech employee arrives for work and enters the office her boss is sitting all by himself in front of his computer: the five other employees are nowhere to be seen. "Where is everyone?" asks the boss. The Czech woman explains that she had a very difficult time getting to work because of snow-related traffic problems. Her boss replies tersely, "That's no excuse for being late! What would our customers think? And what if the Board of Directors came by and saw that no-one was here?" He repeats this to each employee one by one as they arrive late at work. His answer to the explanation that the streets are in absolute chaos due to the enormous snow fall is always the same: in a monotone he states that this is no excuse. He is so relentless in his attitude that one employee begins to cry. He asks her why she is crying. She explains that she really had done her best to get to work on time, but she was stuck in a traffic jam, and that she is shaken that he is treating it so seriously. To this he answers, "Don't take this criticism personally. I just have to insist on punctuality. Just imagine if . . ." Half an hour later when an Austrian colleague finally arrives, he is also taken into the boss's office to be reprimanded. The boss then calls an outlying office, where he himself is expected for an appointment in an hour, and says, "I'm sorry but I'll be arriving a bit late. I had something very important to discuss in the office."

Learning from mistakes that have been pointed out is of significant value according to the logic of internalising rules. Since no-one wants to be seen as being unreliable, sloppy or incompetent, they accept the necessity of life-long "education" that will leave their feelings of self-worth feeling bruised at times. This, it is assumed, will encourage them to make more of an effort and do a better job next time.

The Social Component: Justice and Fairness

The many norms, regulations and agreements that exist in Germany should ideally be adhered to by everyone, resulting in a well-functioning society. Germans do not like making exceptions. Justice for Germans means having the same standards for everyone: all citizens receive the same treatment with regards to opportunities and rights but also to the duties and sanctions. If anyone is granted an exception or some kind of special treatment, Germans consider this to be unfair. Everyone knows what to expect and everyone is treated equally. This, according to popular opinion, prevents corruption, favouritism and unfairness. Moreover, it guarantees an atmosphere of control and predictability. Exceptions could all too easily become dangerous precedents.

A Chinese manager has received a parking ticket. He tells his German colleague about the incident and asks him to put in a good word for him with the authorities, so that he won't have to pay the fine. His German colleague is unwilling to intervene personally. He defends the system and explains to his Chinese colleague that everyone who parks incorrectly gets a ticket and he must pay, otherwise he will be subjected to further legal action (a fine or worse). This holds true even if it is the German Chancellor, a professor, the director of a large company or just an ordinary person. The Chinese manager can't understand why his colleague won't help him.

One could argue about how many Germans, just to be polite, would have taken the parking ticket and just paid it, but this particular German wanted to show a principle: "Everyone is treated equally by the law." The Chinese manager must learn that the observance of laws in Germany is much more strictly enforced than he may be used to, and that personal connections cannot be exploited to avoid legal consequences.

When exceptions are made, there must be an urgent and compelling reason. The person who is asking to be exempted must be evaluated as being very responsible and someone who normally, *and in every other situation,* toes the line. The acceptance of a rule is the prerequisite that it may be ignored *once.*

An important consequence of the culture standard *"Rule-Oriented, Internalised Control"* is Germans' preference for contracts, instead of putting their trust in the relationship. In Germany, observing a contract is not a case of trust or a matter of liking or disliking someone. A signed contract supersedes a basis of trust between business partners, in line with the German emphasis on objective task-orientation rather than subjective person-orientation. Though trust is a prerequisite for the development of many business relationships, it often develops only over the course of time due to the positive experience of working together for a long time on the basis of a contract.

A Chinese manager from a textile company has a business relationship with a large German trading company. As part of an important contract he has promised his customer that the products will be delivered punctually. However, unexpected problems have come up. The Chinese manager tells his customer that, due to the unforeseen problems, the product cannot not be delivered on time. The manager of the German company gets very angry and reminds his business partner about their contract and that he has given them his word. He puts pressure on him to deliver the goods as stipulated, otherwise he will cancel the whole contract. This massive threat is a huge blow to the Chinese manager who feels shocked and alienated.

In summary we can say the following about the German understanding of contracts:
– what was agreed upon and what is written down is what counts;
– contracts are the final product of a mutual process of consent; they are not an intermediate stage in setting up a business relationship (which tends to be the case in Asia);
– no further obligations or long-term relationships will result from contracts;
– negotiations that occur at a later stage are proof that a great deal was forgotten or was not properly dealt with during the original negotiation of the contract. Problems or changes that occur later do not help to further a trusting relationship between partners; rather, they are seen as deficiencies or shortcomings of the party seeking changes.

Independence and Autonomy

Internalisation is learned throughout a person's socialisation process. From a very early age, Germans learn to adhere strictly to rules which are instituted and exemplified by their elders. As they grow older, children learn to internalise these rules and "regulate" themselves in accordance with what they have learnt from experience and example. Raising children in Germany is characterised by helping and convincing children to appreciate the necessity for rules, by appealing to their understanding, insight and intelligence. This is done by explaining the reasons for the prohibitions and demands and allowing the children, depending upon their age, to make their own decisions. Accordingly, "constructive criticism" is seen as more valuable as an educational tool than punishment. Parents, in turn, stand by the agreements they make with their children and will not thoughtlessly go back on their word: a promise is a promise. Later on during school and career, those who have developed personal responsibility will enjoy more success – those who are conscientiously able to meet the demands of explicitly stated rules and unspoken expectations, by applying internalised control.

A mother has a bad headache. Although she had promised to take her children to an amusement park that evening, she has delayed their departure because of her headache, and the children are now grumbling impatiently. Eventually she gives in, "OK, I promised, so I'll take you to the fun park now," and gets up. Her Czech Au Pair is concerned for the sick mother and tells the children, "You should go easy on your mother. With such a bad headache she should stay in bed. You can always go to the park another day." The children complain in unison, "But she promised to take us today!" The Au Pair repeats her statement. Finally, the children think it over and decide to postpone their visit. "It's OK. But we have to go tomorrow!" they tell their mother, who promises "Yes, of course we will."

How does this relate to the workplace? What do independence and autonomy mean on the job?
1. The intentions, tasks and rules detailed in plans, norms or common agreements are taken on and internalised as personal goals.
2. The individual works autonomously towards achieving these goals as fully as possible.
3. If problems occur, appropriate measures are taken to deal with them without someone else having to give instructions or orders.
4. If deemed useful and productive, serious hurdles, desired changes, suggestions for improvements or corrections will be explicitly discussed with the relevant colleagues or superiors.

In combination with displaying independence and autonomy, proper roles must be maintained:

- A person is polite, stays composed and behaves correctly.
- Each person carries out the tasks and duties within their field of competence and authority, respecting boundaries, but at the same time taking advantage of the full range of possibilities.
- With respect to communication style this means that Germans engage in thorough discussions, are prepared to struggle hard to make difficult decisions, and speak with absolute conviction.
- Once an agreement has been reached or an arrangement has been made, everybody expects everybody else to know what they have to do, and further questions seem unnecessary: "no sooner said than done." Further questions to check that everyone is clear may even be considered an insult, implying unreliability.
- Appointments are made to be kept. This is a very deep-rooted rule. When a boss asks one of his employees when something will be ready, the question is not to be taken lightly. And, since employees are considered the experts in their field, they are expected to give realistic and reliable estimates. A boss may change a deadline if there are grounds emanating from a higher level, but an employee is obliged to meet a deadline or any other agreement he has made. For this reason, not only getting the job done but also the very act of setting a deadline in Germany can create stress.
- Perfect job performance is expected. This is why Germans are so willing to invest money and time in good professional training, but they do expect this investment to be worthwhile.
- Employees only go to their bosses when the task at hand is outside their responsibility or when a decision needs to be approved. Otherwise they work independently within their personal area of competence, which is simply what their bosses expect.

This is true in private life as well: everyone is expected to deal with their own issues and tasks. Due to the all-encompassing nature of this culture standard Germans are sometimes considered to be slaves to authority. Most anecdotes told to demonstrate this characteristic are explained, from the German viewpoint, by this culture standard, just as in this example:

A Polish woman is studying at a German university. Her class normally begins at 5:15 p. m. The minutes tick by and the professor doesn't appear! The students begin to discuss whether the class has been cancelled or whether anyone knows why there could possibly be a delay. At 5:30 p. m., the Polish student gathers her things together and announces, "I don't wait more than a quarter of an hour for anyone, not even for a professor." The German students say that surely he'll show up, as otherwise he would have told someone or left a message on the bulletin board. They all wait. The Polish student's belief that Germans are ruled by authority is once again confirmed. The professor does not come. He had become very ill earlier that afternoon. Because he had to go to the doctor immediately, he didn't have time to put a message on the board or to tell someone someone and the office was already closed for the day. At the next class he explains to the students why he hadn't been able to come and apologises.

The students did not wait out of respect for their professor, but because of the "agreement" (the appointment for the class). Because this agreement had not been cancelled, the Germans students continued to assume that everything would go as planned. There are many similar examples of Germans following structures, rules and regulations, agreements and contracts very dutifully, in a very disciplined manner, especially when they have accepted this responsibility voluntarily.

The Obligation to Inform

An integral part of the logic surrounding *internalised control* is the so-called *obligation to inform*. This means that if people run into difficulties completing a task, they have a duty to inform all the parties that are involved, be it the boss, colleagues, or customers. What is expected in these situations is summed up in many German proverbs extolling the virtues of resolving conflicts in personal responsibility by pro-actively reporting the problem. The person who has the problem is expected to organise a problem-solving meeting so that appropriate measures, which take everyone into consideration, can be introduced in time. This course of action can naturally be embarrassing, especially when it is your mistake. This way of handling things, however, is equivalent to showing consideration for one's colleagues and will not be taken as a sign of incompetence, as long as it does not happen regularly. On the contrary, such behaviour is considered conscientious and appropriate treatment of problems. Being honest about difficulties and openly admitting one's mistakes shows a high level of responsibility, self-confidence and reliability. If someone does not mention a problem, but instead tries to hide it, it is inevitable that others will react angrily; they have held up their end of the bargain to work in a self-disciplined and conscientious manner and expect the same. The longer a problem has been kept hidden, the greater the anger. This concept of an *obligation to inform* is so natural and integrated into German thinking that many German bosses do not even consider asking if there are any problems. If they do not hear anything to the contrary, they expect everything to go as planned. They expect each employee to take the initiative themselves, to work independently and to come to them if any problems arise. For the most part German bosses understand their job as managers is to allow their employees as much freedom as possible and to intervene only when an employee is unable to do something independently, which in this context can be understood as upward delegation.

The Moral Value of Rule-Oriented, Internalised Control

The defining characteristics of rule-oriented, internalised control are the measurement of commitment, trustworthiness and the appropriate amount of respect. A strong sense of duty and responsibility to social structures, agreements and roles is expected. Rule-oriented, internalised control is a way of upholding norms with a clearly moralistic touch.

An eighty year old German woman is living in the same apartment house as an expatriate Indian couple. To the Indians' great amazement this woman cleans the stairwell in weekly rotation just like all the other tenants. She is also very active and travels a lot. She is planning a three week holiday and asks her Indian neighbors if they would mind taking over her cleaning duties just during this time. She then takes out a calendar to write down when the Indian couple would normally have to clean so that she can clean for them on those days. The Indian woman is more than happy to stand in for the old lady and doesn't want to swap with her, but the German woman reacts vehemently. If the Indian woman won't agree to the swap with her, she'll have to ask someone else or she can't go away. The Indian woman agrees, and is then totally amazed when, after her trip, the older woman thanks her with a bouquet of flowers. True to her word, she turns up armed with her cleaning equipment on the Monday of the week in which the Indians originally had cleaning duty, determined to argue with them about who gets to do the cleaning. The Indian woman thinks to herself that this is very strange: she is so refined, so educated, not so young any more and yet she still insists on cleaning?

According to the principles of well-bred and respectable Germans, people keep their word, there are no special rules or special treatment, the rules are the same for everyone irrespective of position, age, nationality or relationship. At the same time it *is* also true that these standards are upheld to varying degrees, and can be neglected by most Germans at same time or another, depending on the person or situation. This is often the case when a German is totally unmotivated at work and takes the stance of doing *only* the bare minimum, but that is usually still enough to ensure that the work does not come to a complete standstill.

Unfortunately it would be stretching the truth considerably to say that all Germans admit to their mistakes. Too often they are overconfident about what they are doing, and often they just do not want to be seen as careless, sloppy or incompetent in their field. Clearly, an error is far more serious in a culture such as that of Germany, which is distinguished by its rule-oriented, internalised control, objectivism and planning in order to minimise error, than in a personoriented culture which revolves more around the principle of trial and error. Nevertheless, acknowledging errors which *have* occurred is morally very highly valued in Germany.

The managing director of a Czech company fills out an order form and faxes it to his German partner company. The German managing director has the goods sent to Prague. Instead of the 122 parts that were ordered only 22 arrive. The Czech manager calls Germany and brings the problem to the German's attention, who responds with "Oh God, what have I done! I must have misread it!'" The Czech manager is pleasantly surprised but also perplexed: why does he admit to having made a mistake when he could have just said that the fax was illegible?

The culture standard *"Rule-Oriented, Internalised Control"* reveals the depth of German commitment to their principles: in no way is objectivism equivalent to being heartless or shallow, on the contrary it represents enormous identification and engagement from a motivated person. In fact, some people identify so much with their task or their issues that they do everything possible to achieve success, accepting personal disadvantages along the way and being just as strict and demanding towards others. They may seem to be missionary in their zeal, and can be inconsiderate and almost fanatical. Many non-Germans find it difficult to detect the good intention behind such a hard facade.

This culture standard can also explain the phenomenon of sudden negative emotional outbursts. If someone identifies strongly with their job, any sort of a disturbance can incite them to anger: self-directed anger when the mistake is their own and annoyance with others when it is clear that they have not mustered up the expected discipline and engagement. These feelings of resentment will be expressed more or less depending on the seriousness of the situation as perceived by the individual. In this context, the negative emotion is not rude, but justified. In the end, it is not consideration for others which sets the tone in an encounter, but the obligation to follow norms, rules and agreements. Because of this, Germans are often seen as "misery-gutses," "wet blankets" and generally as grumpy, critical, and even aggressive.

The Pros and Cons of Rule-Oriented, Internalised Control

The great advantage of rule-oriented, internalised control is that Germans are in the position of being able to organise systems unerringly, effectively and reliably because they are able to identify so clearly with their work. This characteristic is valued and acknowledged as truly "professional" by many who see it as typically German. *Germans are reliable. Germans keep their word.*

A disadvantage arises when this characteristic is exaggerated. Sometimes people become so involved in their job that they cannot separate themselves from it, and as a result come across as being uncommunicative, uncompromising, stubborn and even pig-headed. Germans often react to lack of success by being even more rigid about their principles, and sticking even more firmly to structures and agreements. The strong internalisation of plans may lead to an exaggerated conviction that only the German way is the right way. Germans often fail to realise that something could be done differently to how they have planned, with a similar result. In any case, it would be seen as a superficial solution as their work is based on long, carefully planned considerations.

Every so often their love of consensus can put Germans in a weak negotiating position, such as when they regard a result as more binding than the other side and play their best cards early in the negotiation process. For the Germans, the deal may appear to be done when for the others, the game is just beginning. In this regard, Germans are comparatively naïve when carrying out complex negotiations in which they have to represent their own interests.

Recommendations

Suggestions for non-Germans Working with Germans:

- Take rules and frameworks seriously. This enhances your reputation as a colleague and as a person.
- If you are unsure about something, inquire about the rules, norms and standard procedures. Ask someone to help you to understand things that are unclear so that you can work towards a common solution. This will help you to be respected as a conscientious person and you will also be seen as an interested, motivated employee.
- Consult your bosses about problems. They expect this because of their higher level of competence and responsibility. How can your bosses support you so that you can best fulfill your duties? In this case Germans don't regard looking for help as a sign of weakness or an attempt to undermine the boss' authority but rather as a sign of you wanting to do your job well.
- It can actually increase your credibility and the respect you will receive from your bosses if you tell them what you've already done to solve a problem.
- Germans like it when someone shows initiative (and talks about it!)
- Don't try to be nice to your German colleagues by making plans or agreements because they happen to cross your path and you want to do them a favour – *unless* you are absolutely sure that you *can* and *want* to keep your word! Germans see arrangements and acceptances as serious obligations. If you don't stick to your arrangement because you didn't take it seriously but only made it to make the other person feel good then you are only making matters worse. In this situation the German not only feels let down on the objective, task level, but also left in the lurch or even betrayed on the personal, social-emotional level.
- Let someone know if something isn't going as planned. In this

way, Germans have a chance to react and to consider another way to reach their goals. You will also avoid the big clash that will inevitably follow if you fail to reach the goal.

- For Germans it is very important that everybody sticks to their roles. Because of this, it is vital that you're clear about what your role is and what is expected of you. The answer will be the truth: no more, no less.

Suggestions for Germans Working with non-Germans:

- The key to motivating non-Germans is often found on a personal level, and you should remember this in your interaction with them. The typical German way of referring to plans and structures is often counter-productive and comes across as authoritarian.
- When drawing up plans and structures, try to involve everyone so that you can work together towards the common goal. Encourage discussion about changes or actions you are proposing. Ask what could be done and how, and then give others the opportunity to show initiative. Take other people's ideas seriously and don't dismiss them without real discussion. Be prepared to consider two possible paths to a desired outcome. You will be seen as having a good style of communication if you try to develop ideas together instead of lecturing your non-German colleagues: "How could this be done? I suggest we try ... but what do you think? Is that OK with you?" Resistance to new tasks should always be expected. Although it will take more time, really involving people in any change process or cooperative project will convince them of its worth and yield good results. Presenting your own favoured option as *one* alternative which will be considered like the others clears the way for fair discussion.

Historical Background

Through consistent and unflinching rationality, Roman law restricted the central power of the family and clan (Nipperdey 1991), and the law, rather than relationships to particular people, became binding. The law aimed to establish justice. This was its central purpose and encompassed the principles of consistency, clarity and fairness.

As early as Roman times, contracts therefore played a decisive role (Dinzelbacher 1993), and the Roman concept of law eventually spread throughout continental Europe.

Judaism also has God-given social laws which *everyone must obey equally:* the Ten Commandments of the Old Testament were given without justification, but have to be followed without question and without reward. A monotheistic creator-God has sufficient authority to demand this (Cahill 2000). Each person is responsible for his or her own sins, and to act correctly must abide by God's law. The interpretation of the Ten Commandments in relation to specific situations in everyday life was the responsibility of religious leaders, but also of individuals as the voice of God spoke to them through their conscience. The Jewish God is thus not a god of external symbols, but a god of the conscience; demanding no exterior piety, but obedience, the hearts of the people: their inner being (Cahill 2000).

In early Christianity the culture of morality and conscience came to have even greater significance as the Jewish laws were replaced by the command to love God and one's "brothers"; which contributed to transferring the judgement of good or bad to the individual Christian. Thereafter, through increasing missionary work, the institution of the church expounded many cultural and social commands; weakening free decision-making via the conscience, and achieving a measure of internalisation of the church's regulations through the confession of infringements. Protestantism in turn strengthened the development of conscience and the internalisation of authority by eliminating the mediation of the church between God and man (there could be no more institutional granting of forgiveness of sin) and abolished saints as advocates of life hereafter. Each person was now responsible to God and thus above all to his or her conscience (Mensching 1966).

Further aspects have to be considered with regard to the particular formation of the cultural standard *Rule-Oriented, Internalised control* in Germany.

In the early *small states* the rulers and the people were in relatively close contact. This resulted in (a) a greater degree of internalisation of the wishes and commands of the rulers, compared to larger states. This occurred not so much from conviction but because of the sheer inescapability of authority (Molz 1994). Furthermore (b) many princes were far from being despotic. They frequently regarded themselves more in the role of a typical Germanic sovereign lord, who ruled his subjects as a benevolent patriarch, giving protection and security in return for unconditional allegiance (Sana 1986; Kindermann).

So, although the tribes of the German empire adopted the formal and institutional elements of the Greco-Roman legal concept through the centuries, the small size of the territories kept the old ties from completely dissolving. On the contrary, loyalty, laws and sheer inevitability strengthened the readiness to obey rules; as did the horrors of war, in the hope of avoiding such catastrophes in the future, even if it meant exploitation by the protecting lord.

With the rise of absolutism the military and bureaucratic gentry took over rule, putting citizens into second rank after princes, court aristocracy and military noblemen (Elias 1992; Pross 1982). Because the middle-class elite took its cue from the upper-class nobility, military models such as duty and obedience were more readily integrated into the German mind-set. Yet the end of the era of small, territorial states by no means meant the end of the prevalence of the established values of duty and obedience. The unification of Germany, which the middle-classes attempted but failed to achieve in 1848, was successful in 1871 as a result of military action. Emotionally, this constituted a victory for the nobility over the middle-class. Upper-class status still eluded the middle-class industrialists and capitalists but they remained compliant – now within the national state – in the hope of ascent "to the social order of the empire ... adopting its models and norms" (Elias 1992, p. 23; Wagner 1996). An essential factor was the fact that nearly all men had to serve in the military, where they were exposed to basic military values like command and obedience (Pross 1982).

These values were also important in disciplining the masses streaming into the cities due to industrialisation. Production in the factories was likewise organised according to the command and obedience model. The reason why these hierarchical models were accepted in people's work and private lives is also rooted in Protestantism.

Lutheranism, in particular, could have had a decisive influence on the German formation of the *Rule-Oriented, Internalised Control* in two respects: firstly, it forced an internalisation of Christian norms in the sense of a conscience and secondly, it prescribed obedience towards all secular norms.

Luther's introduction of independent Bible study enabled the individual to be more autonomous and independent of theological experts. Henceforth a mediator between God and man was deemed unnecessary. The Protestant tradition regards every individual as a concrete image of the divine spirit, who can only find salvation for himself and through himself (self-control, impulse-control). In Protestantism the freedom of a Christian manifests itself in the *free and voluntary* commitment to the word of God by personal decision (Mensching 1966). People therefore feel ethically responsible for their fate and go about their daily tasks conscientiously (Nuss 1992). For "life is based on conscience and conscience is the conscience of the individual" (Nipperdey 1991, p. 42).

In this context Protestantism saw work as a primary field of Christian "probation," a testing ground, which gave it sanctified status. Work is a divine calling, all professions offer the same opportunities for the testing of faith and worth, (Mensching 1966; Nipperdey 1991) and every individual is obliged by God to perform their duties and tasks for the common good (Troeltsch 1925). "This religious ethic demanded all tasks to be performed with great seriousness, a great deal of care and great concentration, especially those specific to one's profession" (Molz 1994, p. 116). In this respect all people have a calling and are duty-bound to their positions within a traditionally determined social fabric (Münch 1993).

It should be noted that the high regard for professional work and diligence can be traced back to the oldest Christian and patriarchal models of government, although Protestantism provided the detailed theology which lead to their becoming civic virtues as well (Münch 1984). This work ethic resulted in a clear, albeit temporary, lead in economic development of German Protestant areas compared to Catholic areas (Kindermann).

Despite the revolutionary potential of his theology, Luther preached obedience to secular as well as divine authority. Admittedly his original concern had been the abolition of church supremacy over the state. As a monk he sought and found refuge against prosecution by the Pope with his sovereign, Prince Friedrich, Duke of Saxony. Thus, from the outset, Luther's Protestantism was subordinate to the powerful interests of the princes, and the protection granted was repaid by the Protestant legitimisation of obedience (Engelmann 1977; Münch 1993). Luther taught that God guides the world through the secular powers, who therefore command respect. Of course, laws can be changed, but it is not appropriate for a Christian to rebel against them or to put up resistance to political rulers (Nuss 1992; Kalberg 1988).

In summary, personal control and autonomy (conscientiousness) as promoted by Protestantism were enhanced in the course of German history by strong authoritarian and state forces. These two lines of development united in the educational and social reforms of the Prussian state, which brought progress but left the system of absolutism untouched. Under mainly Calvinistic influence in Prussia, subjects became "actively obedient" and "co-responsible citizens" (Böhm 1995, p. 83), obeying the state independently and voluntarily. (Craig 1985). Luther had already demanded that people should not just mechanically perform their tasks but should think for themselves, work well and productively and make the best of all situations. The result in Prussia was that government officials, guided by their conscience, accepted responsibility for the quality of their work. With increasing secularisation the Protestant virtues then became civic ideals (Nipperdey 1991, p. 50) of enthusiasm for work, thrift, humility, endeavour, and material success (Nuss 1992).

In the professional sphere, the Protestant "ethic of conscientiousness" merged with the values of duty and obedience found in the absolutist states (Klages 1987): "Duty was a moral imperative for everyone, from the road-sweeper to the General. . . . It applied to all social relations" (Pross 1982, p. 46). Duty meant self-control *and* performance, service *and* concrete competence, commanded only by one's own conscience (Pross 1982). State ethics argued that obedience and belonging safeguards harmony and a functioning community. According to this philosophy disturbances had their origin in human weaknesses and faults that had to be overcome to ensure the well-being of the community.

Even representatives of workers and social democrats regarded discipline and obedience as virtues and appreciated order (Pross 1982). The growing class consciousness in Germany did not lead to revolts as in other countries, but increased the level of organisation of workers.

These Protestant values eventually reached the Catholic areas of Germany as well because, during the Counter-Reformation, the faiths not only competed with one another on the battlefield but also in the classroom and in pastoral work. Catholicism was consequently also reformed internally and religiousness in general increased (Bausinger 2000; Kindermann).

This model was further strengthened by the economic upswing between 1871 and 1914 because it appeared to provide proof that authoritarian structures were efficient! (Pross 1982). Diligence facilitated social advancement (Gelfert 1983) and that required personal initiative and self-discipline (Molz 1994). The Germans were motivated to catch up with and join their European neighbours: an eminently profound, positive *existential* experience (Kindermann).

The First World War, its battles and the associated material struggles transferred this ethic to an entirely new situation. Many divisions were destroyed by the individual and collective hardships brought about by war, traditional separations resulting from class, milieu, religion and ideology were diminished and put into context (something welcomed by many), and a new sense of national unity developed. Yet the ideals of duty and obedience survived and were, in fact, further strengthened (Klages 1987).

These unquestioned values of duty and obedience contributed greatly to the catastrophe of the Nazi-dictatorship and the Second World War. The crimes and horrors of this war were indescribable for all concerned and a radical turning point in German history. How does this scenario of values present itself today? Has something changed? The answer is both yes and no.

No: in the years after the war there was a massive re-affirmation of the sense of *duty* (Klages 1987) with the reconstruction of bombed German cities. The restoration of an orderly, technical-economic functionality was overwhelmingly evident. "And it was obvious that personal daily co-operation ... in the sense of a conscientious assumption and enacting of one's role was called for." "Order" and "performance of one's duty" were basic human values in the most immediate sense imaginable. Raising efficiency and effectiveness likewise formed an integral part of the value systems of the reconstruction period (Klages 1987, p. 216). Values centered on *rule-orientated control* were decisive "... the will to co-operate, to submit to an overall binding model ..." (Sauzay 1986, p. 59).

Yes: authoritarian values *(obedience),* demanded in public life for centuries and supported by training in the school and family, were changed for good after the Second World War. The shock of discovering that the Nazi terror was made possible, amongst other things, by these very values and mentality raised doubts and unsettled the Germans much more than was realised by the world outside. As a result, self-development increased in importance and independence became one of the essential goals of education. Children should "not become pliant, not be prepared to be obedient and subordinate without question" (Pross 1982, p. 85), but must stand their ground, assert themselves, exercise their rights, not let themselves be trodden on. Independence means the ability to judge, critical faculties, self-confidence, having a will of one's own, and competitiveness.

Yes and no: on the other hand, according to educational research, children must acquire task-based and relevant capabilities and skills. This is where old virtues come into their own: "The acquisition of knowledge requires order, discipline, self-restraint. Without these ... highly esteemed competence is not attainable" (Pross 1982, p. 88). Competence and efficiency therefore have remained educational goals, *but* they should "above all serve the individual and his happiness, his interests and not a higher cause ..." (Pross 1982, p. 88). The traditional value of *diligence* now has a non-traditional association with the value *personal independence* (as opposed to blind obedience previously): independence and self-reliance shall be acquired by experience and performance. Work has likewise lost its status as life's purpose and is now perceived as an instrumental activity. Nevertheless, for a large majority of people, work remains a "source of self-esteem, origin of gratification, means to social contact, basis of status" (Pross 1982, p. 95). Yet one constant factor remains: a basic distrust of authorities, also in the professional field. According to opinion polls, no other (Western-) European nation so consistently demands self-justification from its authorities. Regulations must be justified by insight (Noelle-Neumann 1987).

Concisely formulated, this scenario of values today means that obedience is out, but discipline is not. Today we find "values of duty, acceptance and self-development in large sections of the population" (Klages 1987, p. 222). To achieve success one has to work in a profoundly rule-orientated and internally-controlled manner, thereby making one's own good fortune. The external perception of Germans as being *slaves to authority* is accurate as far as the historical development of the phenomena goes, but no longer reflects the self-definition of modern Germans. Today, Germans are willing to accept discipline, but only *after* basic consent to a particular matter, agreement, or structure is reached. Without this consent, expressed on the basis of personal interests or insights into an arbitrary "matter," discipline has become very brittle.

These contradictory values of *duty* and *self-development* represent the psychological manifestations of different development phases in Germany, forming a mix "that disallows the formation of a specific and lasting 'identity' of the people" (Klages, 1987, p. 223): the meaning of this is dealt with in the chapter on *"Differentiation of Personality and Living Spheres."*

Time Planning

■ Time Planning

How Germans are perceived by other cultures	
punctual at work and in private life	*Australians, Belgians, British, French, Indians, Japanese, Koreans, Poles, Portuguese, South Africans, Czechs, Hungarians*
appointments are always required (in private life too). Life is dictated by the schedule planner, no spontaneity, receiving or entertaining guests requires prior arrangement	*Brazilians, British, Chinese, Indians, Japanese, Koreans, Poles, Spaniards, Hungarians, Taiwanese, Turks*
regulated periods of rest, boring Sundays	*Australians, Chinese, British, Japanese*
strict opening times for everything (doctors, stores, offices)	*Australians, Chinese, French, Japanese, Mexicans, Portuguese, Swedes, Singaporeans, Taiwanese, Americans*
unnecessarily impatient	*Brazilians, French, Indians, Spaniards*
goal-oriented	*Spaniards, Czechs, Hungarians*
work sequentially, only do one thing at a time (but do that very exactly)	*Australians, Indians*
work slowly but thoroughly; minimal stress at work	*Indians, Italians, Poles, Spaniards, Taiwanese, Turks, US-Americans*
set breaks for small talk, then concentrate on work again	*French*
keep appointments	*Turks*
short working hours	*Indians, Japanese, Mexicans*
never enough time, always in a hurry	*Chinese, Russians*
vacation is long, sacred and unalterable; breaks and the end of the work day are important	*Japanese, Koreans, Spaniards*
leisure time is planned down to the last detail, always occupied, relaxation is coupled with some activity (for example, sport)	*Mexicans, Poles, Hungarians, Turks*

121

Time can be structured and used in many different ways. There are cultures in which people make rough plans and then act spontaneously depending on the situation. They take things as they come and react by adapting to what appears to them to be the important needs in the here and now. Thus, they alternate between different courses of action often and quickly, sometimes following an only roughly defined goal or fulfilling some short-term requirements. From the outside, their behaviour does not seem to be planned, but instead quite spontaneous. People from these cultures plan their time less than Germans, and are used to dealing with tasks according to the actual level of urgency they perceive.

On the other hand, there are cultures in which people draw up considerably more detailed timelines and structure each step (for example, by scheduling discussions) in order to reach their goals. They put a great deal of effort into carrying out their plans as well as they can, and persist with whatever plan of action has been allocated to a particular period of time. They concentrate at a particular time on a particular thing. To an outsider, this behaviour appears to be well-planned, although it is also relatively inflexible. The latter characterises the way Germans tend to deal with their time.

Definition of Time Planning

An American woman is working in a German research lab. She repeatedly experiences knock backs when she asks her German colleagues if they'd like to go to a pub, party or concert in the evening with her. To her surprise she hears answers like, "Sorry, I can't, I have to be at the lab again very early tomorrow and want to go to bed early," or they have to do the housework or some gardening. One colleague even told her that he wouldn't be available at any time in the next two weeks since he was writing an article for a publication about his research findings. The American can't understand this German behaviour.

The Chinese manager of a textile firm tries again and again to invite a German colleague to dinner after work. The German declines his invitations over and over again with words like, "Sorry but I'm all booked out this evening, my schedule planner is full. Maybe we could make a date for next week." This method of planning so far in advance causes problems for the Chinese manager. He wonders if it is all a strategy to keep him at a distance. In fact, he is confused about what it all means. He is frustrated by how difficult it is to get to know and be accepted by Germans.

A professor from Prague has been invited to visit a German university. The most important appointments have long been arranged. A week before his visit, he receives a detailed schedule, listing whom he will meet and when, for how long, the room numbers for the meetings, directions for finding the university and so on Since he has already been to Germany several times he knows that his visit will in fact follow this detailed schedule. One the one hand, he likes the fact that he can depend on things going just as planned, but on the other hand, it restricts his freedom. On a particular day he is supposed to be at an office at 10 a. m., to get a certain form. If he can't be there at exactly the right time, he knows he shouldn't expect to get the form. Therefore, whatever he wants to do must be planned around the given schedule.

A Japanese man requires a German driver's licence, which he applies for at the District Administration Office. They tell him he can get his licence quickly if he brings a photo of himself and a translation of his Japanese driver's licence. When he comes to the office a second time with both documents he is told that he needs an official translation, and that the one he has is not sufficient. "Where do I get it?" " At the ADAC." "Where is the ADAC?" "You'll have to look in the telephone directory." At the ADAC he is told that the translation will take a week. After a week they say they are sorry, but the Japanese translation will take longer; he should come back in a month. Finally, back at the District Administration Office he is told, "Good, you now have everything together. It will now take another month to get the driver's licence because it's the peak holiday time and everyone's away."

The future Spanish production manager is working at the headquarters of his company in Germany for a year doing advanced training. He has been incorporated into the team that deals with the German client who will be purchasing products from his factory back in Spain. To the Spaniard's amazement, meetings with clients are arranged two months in advance. An earlier date is not possible for those involved.

Time is of vital importance to Germans; more than other cultures, they seem to be completely engrossed in their schedule planners and diaries and obsessive about appointments and time planning. All in all, the way they deal with time is extremely inflexible. The positive side of all of this is that when you make an appointment or an arrangement with a German, you can almost always depend on it being kept. The fact is that time is a valuable asset for Germans, and they feel that it should not be wasted, but rather used as effectively as possible. For this reason they prefer to plan their time far in advance, making exacting schedules and then following them precisely. When something needs to be done, there is no time for trivialities! It is much more important to deal with the essentials and not get distracted.

But what do Germans understand by "essentials"?

The Task as the Central Factor in Time Planning

We are already familiar with the central component of this definition from the chapter on *"Objectivism":* whatever is important to getting the task done is *essential.* A schedule should support progress towards the goal on the task level, minimising disturbances and maximising engagement and success. With this in mind, people go quickly and directly to the point without superfluous small talk. They draw up daily schedules and organise agendas for meetings. They take minutes and request confirmation of their acceptance. When problems arise they are dealt with systematically, in an order that is logical (to Germans): firstly, the causes are discussed; secondly, suggestions for solutions are sought; and only thirdly is a step-by-step implementation of the chosen solution delegated to the responsible people. In many cases, the pressure inherent in the problem causes self-inflicted time-pressure.

The Importance of Consecutive Steps in Time Planning

There is a very strong tendency to act according to a step-by-step plan. The only exceptions allowed are for emergencies and necessary breaks such as holidays.

For long-term projects this means that all the work necessary for achieving the goal is divided into steps which are planned in advance, even allowing for setbacks and problems so that each step of the job can be finished on time and without a rush. This is why Germans often hold meetings several weeks or even months before starting work on something. They want to consider everything in their own time and not run the risk of making last minute mistakes because something was overlooked. Germans do not like doing things sloppily because of time pressure.

124

People from other cultures often see Germans as being slow or as worrying unnecessarily about things in the distant future.

Germans tend to display a relatively constant motivation throughout the course of a project. They feel at ease when they have a sensible and realistic time-line. They prefer to work at a steady pace which enables them to keep up-to-date and helps them to avoid making mistakes.

Germans often concentrate on one task at a time and apply themselves to another task only when the first one has been brought to a reasonable, although sometimes interim, conclusion. Doing several things at the same time – multi-tasking – is seen to be stressful and is avoided wherever possible.

A Japanese man wants to buy a clock in Germany. He enters a shop on his way to catch a train. The salesman is in the middle of serving another customer and keeps the Japanese man waiting. He does so patiently, although every now and again he tries to talk to the salesman as he has a train to catch. But every time the salesman reacts with remarks like "Yes, right away" or "One moment please." In the end it's too late, and the Japanese man leaves without having bought a clock to catch his train.

A Brazilian production engineer needs information from the workers about the machines they are currently working on, so he goes for a walk through the production facility. Each time the Brazilian speaks to one of the workers, the worker stops what he is doing, turns to the Brazilian and talks to him. Production begins to flag, and very soon the German boss comes and warns the Brazilian production engineer not to disrupt his men in their work. The Brazilian doesn't understand the problem: "Why can't they give me an answer whilst they're working? They don't have to stop!" he thinks to himself.

A Korean employee wants to speak to his new German colleague. He goes into his office but the German is on the phone. The Korean steps forward and expects a short greeting, but the German doesn't greet him or pay him any attention until he is finished on the phone. The Korean colleague feels he has been treated rudely and is offended.

An English woman is working as a teacher at a German school. In her first year of employment she doesn't yet understand how to calculate grades for report-cards, so she decides to ask a colleague whilst they're sitting together at lunch. The colleague briefly stops eating and asks if the question can wait until he's finished his break, as he's eating right now. After he has eaten the last bite he turns to her and with great readiness to help explains to her what she has to do.

A Polish woman characterises her negotiations with Germans as follows: Germans always have a plan. Right from the start they state which points they want to deal with, and this is what they do, in the right order. If something comes up that is meant to be dealt with later in the agenda, even if it's relevant to the current point, they say, "We'll talk about that later." The Polish woman finds this style of discussion really strange.

When Germans have a goal, they pursue it by organising their actions in a straight line directed straight towards achieving this goal. "Detours" such as delays, interventions or dealing with side-issues are only accepted in exceptional cases. Germans want to finish whatever they have begun and bring their plans to fruition. Only in the case of serious obstacles will they deviate – temporarily – from a plan.

"Germans are conscientious, accurate and painstaking," says a French woman who lives in Germany. They seem to prefer finishing something off today instead of leaving it for tomorrow, or staying in the office for half an hour extra on Friday afternoon instead of taking something home over the weekend. Normally, her German colleagues finish punctually, but when they haven't yet finished what they had planned to finish it's no problem for them to work half an hour or even an hour longer. They are seemingly happy when they finish something.

Not only are plans consistently followed, but problems that arise along the way are also analysed and broken down into workable parts that are then taken care of gradually. Plans involving a company strategy are drawn up on a long-term basis. Short-term profits will be sacrificed for the longer-term success and health of the company.

For Germans, it would be optimal to be able to organise all facets of life consecutively: (1) to think about the issue at hand and make a plan; (2) to put these plans into action without interruptions or disturbances so as to (3) eventually achieve the set goals. Whenever possible, this is exactly how Germans *do* work: they work continuously at a steady pace, and in the end are pleased that it was "really pleasant work."

Appointments as Regulators Between Tasks and People

Germans have the reputation for making and having appointments for anything and everything: at work, for getting together socially, for the hairdressers or for going to the doctor. In Germany, it seems that virtually nothing is possible without having first made an appointment. Spontaneity can be considered unsuitable and annoying, and people who act spontaneously may find themselves snubbed.

A Japanese employee has a suggestion regarding the production area. He approaches his German colleague who replies, "Let's talk about it tomorrow." The Japanese man waits politely for the whole of the next day without bringing up his suggestion. His German colleague doesn't refer to the matter either. Nothing happens, so the Japanese man goes to his boss in the evening and asks to discuss it. The boss says, "Okay, come back tomorrow at 11 a. m.," The meeting takes place as planned. The Japanese man thinks to himself that Germans really aren't at all helpful, but actually quite inconsiderate: they can only work if they can do something from beginning to end without interruption.

In order to get an idea of the headquarter's operations in Germany, a Spanish manager who will eventually manage production in Spain is given a project list with the names of those colleagues with special responsibilities. He takes the list, looks for the first department, and unannounced (!) goes up to a German colleague. The German looks at the Spaniard in surprise and says that unfortunately he doesn't have time right now for his questions. He more or less ignores him since he is busy talking to someone else at that moment regarding an ongoing project. The Spanish manager has the same experience with the next person and with the third one as well. He returns to his office irritated and disappointed and consults one of his colleagues, who advises him to call all the people he wishes to talk to and make appointments with them. After many weeks of waiting and appointment juggling the Spaniard gets most of the information and answers he needs, but even after 3 months he still hasn't managed to talk in person to all of the colleagues on his list.

When Germans cling desperately to their time plans they are, of course, seen as being *anything* but flexible. They continually upset people from other cultures when they say, "I don't have time now," regardless of whether they mean that exact moment in time, today, tomorrow or this week.

A French worker goes to the office of her German colleague, with whom she gets on well and has a friendly relationship, just to have a chat. She sticks her head in the door and asks if her colleague has time at the moment. The German woman answers, "No, not right now," and turns around again. The French woman is dumbfounded. For the rest of the day she mulls over what she could have done to offend her German colleague to make her react in this way.

A Japanese manager of a computer firm gets a visit from his firm's general manager who wants to conduct negotiations with their German business partners. The secretary tries to organise a meeting with the Germans. This doesn't work out since she is trying to arrange it at short notice and the Germans can't find any openings in their schedules. The Japanese general manager is displeased with his employees and dumbstruck over the negative reply from the Germans which he sees as rudeness. The Japanese manager is also perplexed by the behaviour of the Germans since his boss is an extremely important person for whom, he thinks, everyone should always have time.

What gives rise to these situations in which Germans are seen as curt, rude and insulting? Why do Germans act like this? They certainly do not realise that they are causing injury and offence, *because in the German logic of organising time, the feeling of being socially responsible is coupled with time planning.* Germans consider themselves to be following their duty to others by sticking to the time plan. Schedules and appointments have a fundamental social function. As Germans see it, everyone is incorporated into certain plans. The appointments agreed upon by those involved act to cement all common activities because they interlink everyone's schedules and time plans. In agreement with the cultural standard of *objectivism*, individual spontaneous needs, wishes and ideas have to take second place to tasks and goals which are regulated by appointments. The present, with all its "here and now" possibilities, must defer to a painstakingly planned future. On the other hand, when Germans make an appointment they dedicate themselves completely to their partner! The time is then really reserved for the person and matter at hand. After all, anything else would be very rude!

Being punctual and keeping appointments not only ensures that work gets done relatively free of problems, but also protects relationships on the social-emotional level. When someone puts effort into being punctual and reliable, they are proving themselves to be considerate by not causing other people unnecessary inconvenience. Being late, on the other hand, is seen as disrespectful to both the matter at hand and the people involved, since delays may upset their entire time planning and leave less time for other obligations.

Punctuality is one of the most important factors in building trust, and its contribution to creating an image of reliability, engagedness and professionalism cannot be over-rated. Being punctual means observing the time agreed on in the original arrangement. Any changes have to be checked and incorporated into new arrangements.

Polish companies find it hard to deal with the expectation that all delivery dates must be strictly adhered to. The delivery of a batch of goods has been arranged for a certain date. Once again the Germans want to make some changes to the goods and the Poles agree. These changes take extra time, and as a result, the delivery arrives in Germany a few days later than the agreed date. The Germans are displeased, and threaten to reduce the payment as compensation for the delay. This really annoys the Poles: "Firstly, the Germans overwhelm us with changes, then they punish us because we, of course, can't meet the deadline!"

Interruptions and disturbances, except when they cannot be avoided because of substantial problems, can be seen as a signal of contempt towards a person, since their time, which is valuable and has already planned in advance, is being sacrificed.

Germans consider a long warm-up phase in business meetings and discussions to be a waste of time. Getting to the point quickly is a way of showing respect for the precious time of colleagues.

Anyone arriving late should have a very good excuse, otherwise it is clearly seen as an insult. When there is an unavoidable delay (something that happens *even* to Germans more frequently than they would like) it is advisable to inform everyone as quickly as possible so that a solution can be found (together) for the emerging problem. Professional (and very often also private) time planning and appointments are obligatory. If they are not taken seriously, the whole system would come apart at the seams, as others have already based their plans on the fact that each appointment or time plan *will* be kept. Unpunctual people are not just annoying, they also cause concrete difficulties; for example, a supplier being late causes the company waiting for the delivery problems with their customers. If they in turn have customers, the chain of inconvenience and disappointment continues. Because so many obligations and responsibilities ride on the keeping of plans, disturbances in a planned or established course of action can cause anger and substantial, if not massive, problems. For this reason, getting a job done on time and according to plan, and dealing with the task level first, is of the utmost importance and has priority over a personal interests and needs. A full appointment book or schedule planner does not allow for anything spontaneous like short-notice meetings, conversations or visits; and this is why (almost) everything in Germany requires an appointment, even for leisure activities or doctor's visits.

Time has an enormous symbolic value in both the business and social spheres of life. It represents the importance of a matter and/or a person: time is devoted to important matters and to important people. In the working environment, representatives from different departments or companies do not meet together without some real necessity or a clear objective in mind, but rather usually to work together to reach a common goal, or sometimes, to cultivate an important relationship, for example by a business dinner. In their private lives, very busy people only share their precious free time with those who are very meaningful to them. Time is used as a valuable resource, for special purposes. Warm-ups and small talk can thus be seen as a waste of time.

Sometimes, however, there is an ugly side to the German attitude towards time and punctuality: for some bosses, being chronically late is a way of "flexing their muscles" and demonstrating power. This behaviour is nevertheless considered rude, regardless of position, and cannot be regularly justified by them having other urgent appointments.

Time Planning in Private Life

The time allocated to work and the time allocated to private life is adhered to as strictly as possible. Closing time *really is* closing time.

The Chinese manager of a toy company asks his Chinese and German workers to do over-time in the evening as otherwise a job will not be finished on time. The Chinese workers are immediately more than willing whereas the Germans bluntly refuse. They argue that they have worked intensively for 8 hours for the company and after these 8 hours they are entitled to go home and they would then like to organise their free time themselves. The Germans stress that they have families and would like to spend their free time with them. Besides that, they also have a lot to do at home. To stress this point, one of the Germans says that he has promised his wife to look after the children so that she can go to an important appointment. That's why he can't possibly stay! The Chinese manager doesn't know how to deal with the situation.

Time planning continues well into private life. Time has to be used effectively, in order to make the most of it and be able to indulge in leisure and free time activities. Everyone owes this to their families, friends, acquaintances and themselves (for example, in order to stay fit and healthy).

An American studying in Germany asks a German fellow student if she would like to go out for a beer. She declines, saying she is sorry, but she "has to" go riding as she has already made her riding appointment. It occurs to him that his other German acquaintances also almost always have something to do, either for their studies, their hobbies, or they have already arranged to meet friends, and so on. He finds it typical that she has reacted in this way: no-one ever seems to have time, everyone always "has to" do something. If he really thinks about, even his German girlfriend often makes an "appointment" with him, and this really does disappoint him.

The time of finishing work for the day is important to Germans. As a result, the evening seems to be just as planned as the weekend is. At the office, everyone tells each other what they are going to do after work or on the weekend: mow the lawn, plant flowers, clean windows, go on a weekend outing, and so on. For example, the female colleague of a French woman living in Germany always finishes punctually on Friday because on Fridays she always cleans her house. If someone doesn't manage to do what they have set out to do, they also share this at the office and complain about it. If they are not able to stick to their time plans, they seem to get very edgy. The French woman can't wait to hear the next story, because she finds them so amusing.

A single American living in Germany has met a German at a seminar and become friends with him. The German lives in a city in southern Germany. Because the American has said he wants to see as much of Germany as possible, the German frequently invites him to visit him. So far, every weekend that the American has spent at his friend's house has followed a similar pattern: he is received with a meal, then he is told what the plan for this weekend is and asked whether he has any special requests to add. Then they go sleep so that they can get up early the next day to start the day's excursion: a hike in the mountains, a bike ride, or sightseeing. The German always knows the way, even knows all of the best places to stop for a meal, and has booked a place to stay for the night. After getting back on Sunday they always have coffee and cake. He is then asked what he would like to do next time he comes. Would he rather go to the mountains, bike-riding or sightseeing? For each suggestion his German friend already has an idea (and presumably a plan) in reserve. Then the American guest goes home. That there seems to be a clear format for the whole visit appears quite odd to the American.

Time Management

Germans have a well-developed awareness of time and according to the German way of thinking, time management is a prerequisite for effective action and an essential component of professionalism. Employees must be in the position to set themselves time-lines for the tasks within their area of responsibility, make realistic estimates of the time needed for each step, and then discipline themselves to stick to the plan. Time management as an essential prerequisite for fulfilling professional responsibilities is taught in seminars, is part of personnel assessments and it is checked by auditors. Germans allot time for certain actions, like to be able to concentrate on certain things at certain times, and do not want to be disturbed in the process.

There are, of course, a great many activities that do not allow Germans the opportunity to plan ahead, but rather have to be dealt with ad-hoc. In such situations, they naturally *do* manage to get their work done, although they constantly describe themselves as having to "rush around madly." It upsets them greatly if their working schedules simply do not function, and they end up constantly apologising for their lateness and unreliability. They feel compelled to do this otherwise they fear their relationships will suffer and their behaviour will be seen as disrespectful.

In Germany the ideal is clear: time should be planned as well as possible. When one has to juggle time demands from the "task level" and the "social-emotional level," the following is true: "First work, then fun." In accordance with the cultural standard of *"Separation of Personality and Living Spheres"* these two elements are are prioritised: first comes the job and afterwards the small talk. First someone has to prove themselves as a reliable colleague, then friendship can follow. First you have to work towards the goal, then you can celebrate! Many non-Germans formulate it like this: you earn a German's affection by first working hard.

Disturbances and Interruptions

Events that happen unexpectedly are regarded as disturbances, and cause, in the broadest sense, problems and stress which completely throw Germans off balance. The adjustment necessary to correct each disturbance costs a considerable amount of energy. Germans therefore get angry if foreseeable things are inadequately and poorly planned for. In such cases foreigners may view Germans as being inflexible, incapable of improvisation and likely to panic when things do not go according to plan.

A Czech woman working in the hotel industry in Germany is completely astonished by her normally efficient German colleagues. A tour group has come back one and a half hours earlier than expected from an excursion. They ask to be served their meal earlier in order to go to the theatre as tickets have become available. This, too, was not originally planned. The hotel agrees, but behind the scenes, panic breaks out everywhere. The Czech woman sees the chaos and confusion, and her impression of her colleagues as professionals is blown away.

Violations of Time Planning

When *do* Germans overturn or revise their time plans? The answer may amaze you: they do it all the time. If you ask a German, they will say they have the feeling that their plans are always being interrupted and disturbed, nothing functions as it should, and they are permanently in crisis-management and repair mode. In truth, Germans are always lagging behind their plans. Whether a foreigner would actually notice this is, however, questionable. There is usually an immense gulf between Germans' concepts of when something is functioning really well and reality. Paradoxically, this actually supports my explanation of *time-planning*. The scheduling of time is an *ideal* that Germans pursue, but rarely achieve. This path of organising time is a well trodden one, and the end is rarely reached, but along the way, Germans invest a great deal of energy in the pursuit of the ideal.

The term used in time management seminars for the rescheduling of plans is prioritising. Germans will spontaneously alter their plans in view of priorities that are absolutely pressing and so contravene their otherwise highly valued appointment keeping. Such changes are also done methodically. This is how Germans define flexibility: the most urgent thing gets done first, then come all the tasks that are less important. For Germans, prioritising is just another time planning tool.

In a Hungarian plant an audit is planned for six week's time. In preparation, the German manager gives the Hungarians a plan of which tasks have to be completed by which week. In the first week the Hungarians have other things to do, and the same goes for the second week. The German points out again and again everything that has to be done, and that they are falling more and more behind. In the meantime the Hungarians have started working on the first point on the list (out of a total of forty points). A week before the audit they are working on the second point. The German is completely beside himself. If they keep going at this rate, it will be impossible to complete the list of tasks before the audit takes place! He reacts by changing the list completely, now detailing fewer tasks that have to be done and simply dropping others. The Hungarians are completely perplexed. What? Were the original points important or not?

When difficulties arise in production, which is quite common, a complete change of plans is necessary. Those responsible drop all other plans in order to remedy the problem and ignore all their other duties. Afterwards they resume what they were doing.

Social (so-called "soft") arrangements may be cancelled at short notice in favour of more objective, work-related ("harder") obligations. Meetings and training seminars are postponed without hesitation when important tasks arise that must be completed immediately. Getting the job done always wins out over social responsibilities in the battle for time.

Pros and Cons of the Culture Standard "Time Planning"

One advantage of the culture standard of *"Time Planning"* is that because of the attention given to each essential element of a particular task, few things run the risk of being completely overseen or skipped due to time pressure.

A disadvantage is certainly the low level of flexibility: Germans run into difficulties when they feel they have been thrown off their schedule. Because all of their plans are interlinked with each other as well as with those of other people, Germans cannot react flexibly without becoming negligent toward their other agreements and appearing unreliable to other people.

The fixation with time planning has a further disadvantage: it restricts social life. Germans suffer chronically from a lack of time, try to squeeze as much as possible into each day and therefore feel constantly stressed. "But I don't have any time..." is an often heard excuse. For those who feel similarly it is also an acceptable one. In most cases it is not meant at all personally and is not being used as an excuse to avoid someone.

Recommendations

Suggestions for non-Germans Working with Germans

- Stick to the appointments that you have arranged with Germans and notify them as soon as possible of any delays. Conflict will certainly arise if appointments are taken lightly. This is considered unacceptable behaviour.
- Arrange an appointment or a meeting when you want to discuss something. If you try to speak spontaneously with a German, prepare for disappointment, as there is a good chance that you will either be regarded as a trouble-maker, turned away or dealt with quickly because of the lack of time. To arrange an appointment it is enough to say, "I want to discuss this or that matter with you. Do you have time to talk it over now or would another time be better? If not now, when?"
- Take agendas for meetings seriously and make sure that your topics and concerns are taken into consideration and put on the to-do-list.
- Make appointments in your daily life as well, for private visits and invitations, just as you would for more formal matters.
- Be prepared to have a German's undivided attention once you have finally made an appointment with them. Now they have time for you. It would be insulting or rude if they were to be doing something else at the same time. This is true both at work and in private life.
- Don't expect Germans to be flexible. They will do things in a consecutive order and often say to you "Slow down. One thing after the other."
- Be aware that Germans don't change their decisions very quickly once they have been made, so make sure you contribute your ideas and suggestions at the beginning during the planning stage.

Recommendations for Germans Working with non-Germans
- Don't expect extreme punctuality from non-Germans.
- To be on the safe side, plan extra time into your time schedule right from the start (but keep this to yourself!).
- If you absolutely have to get something done, use "follow-ups" and reminders. Explain your situation and obligations clearly and try to demonstrate why the job is urgent and important. Remember: an expression for "a particular point in time," or "Zeitpunkt" does not even exist in some languages. For some people it is absolutely inconceivable that a finishing date could create so much pressure.
- Be aware that saying "I don't have any time …" is a resounding slap in the face for many people from different cultures. They have no understanding or explanation for this behaviour.

Historical Background

Time planning is generally based on a linear perception of time, which is indeed the only way in which it makes sense. Where does this notion come from in Western cultures? The concept of a course of events unfolding step-by-step as a consequence of time was introduced by Judaism. The Jews broke with cyclical thinking (Cahill 2000), since the Jewish god is considered real and not an archaic relic: he truly intervenes in the course of events and changes it. Thus, the perception that history consists of recurring cycles lost its credibility. The monotheistic creator God is active. This is the religious experience of the Jewish people as recorded by them in the Bible. The process is also purposeful although no-one can say what that purpose is. Christianity adopted this perception in the concept of the story of salvation (Nipperdey 1991). The notion of the weekend, for instance, is a Judeo-Christian institution prescribing that one day of rest should be used for prayer, study and recreation.

In Germany, the culture standard of *"Time Planning"* is a by-product (in time form) of *"The Appreciation for Rules, Regulations and Structures"* and should be interpreted as a further consequence of the historical conditions set out in that chapter. The following arguments about the nature of time planning from an historical perspective may be found in the relevant literature.

Life in the *small* German *states* depended on the structuring of time, starting at the latest when the absolutist, enlightened states demanded that citizens strictly regulate their daily routines. They enforced a "comparatively narrow-minded and inflexible organisation of time " (Althaus et al. 1992b, p. 78) via social and political regulations.

Protestantism also contributed to the concept of linear rather than cyclical time, with the casting off of cult worship and the belief in personal responsibility for actions and outcomes (Mensching 1966). There is the image of each person standing alone before their Creator on Judgement Day, having to justify their life and the path they chose, with no "ifs" and "buts." This means time on earth is short, and must be planned for and used well! While Christianity, as opposed to other religions, generally supports the linear concept of time (there is only *one* life and one Judgement Day and one's fate in the hereafter is determined accordingly), Protestantism, in particular, intensified this tendency.

Because the transition from an agricultural to an industrial society occurred earlier in the Protestant areas of Europe and North America than in Catholic areas or in areas with predominantly other religious denominations (Protestantism is regarded as one of the roots of capitalism), the use of time in consecutive steps and linear time-planning was doubly strengthened, as the industrial method of production also required this model. The first wave of industrialisation did not come to Germany until the 19th century, but when it did come it was all the more extensive and successful. Since that time the Germans' interpretation of the conditions of a free market has come to include exact time planning. Proof of this was provided by the economic successes and social upturns of the early 19th century and post Second World War period.

Agenda

■ Separation of Personality and Living Spheres

How Germans are perceived by other cultures	
correct on the job and perform their role perfectly, albeit neutrally, impersonally and unemotionally	*Indians, Poles, South Africans, Czechs, Hungarians*
informal discussions are difficult	*Indians*
don't smile at anyone in the street sales people don't smile at customers	*British* *Japanese*
not much conversation in the workplace	*French, Indians, Russians, Turks*
in public (at work and in everyday life): only a few are friendly, most are not nice, unemotional, little small-talk *at work:* colleagues are often friendly and likeable *in private:* when you get to know them they are very nice, hospitable, willing to help	*Indians, Japanese, Mexicans, US Americans*
a colleague is not a friend (even if he's friendly)	*Brazilians, Indians, Indonesians, Japanese, Spanish, Turks*
life takes place in the home, don't go out very much, very private	*Brazilians, British, Spanish*
oriented towards holidays and free time; weekends and the end of the working day are distinct boundaries	*Chinese, Finns, Indians, Italians, Singaporeans*
loosen up at parties	*Indians*
marked roles for men and women: child *or* career, no combination of the two (because childcare provision is lacking), no female engineers, bosses are always men	*French, Dutch, Poles, Swedes, Spanish Indians, Belgians, British, Dutch*
often in a bad mood, unsatisfied, not positive, unhappy, complain a lot	*Brazilians, Indians, South Africans, Spanish, Turks, US-Americans*

they act superior, boastful, condescending, conceited, arrogant	*Bulgarians, Chinese, French, Poles, Swedes, Swiss, Czechs, Hungarians*
little contact between people, distant, reserved, formal, cold, not open, restrained, little small-talk, polite (but not warm), careful; making friends is difficult	*Australians, Brazilians, Bulgarians, Chinese, Indians, Italians, Mexicans, Spanish, Czechs, Turks, Hungarians, US Americans*
hardly any contact between neighbours	*Brazilians, Indians, Turks*
very formal: Du/Sie (the familiar and polite forms of "you"), use of title and surname: Herr X/Frau Y	*Australians, Belgians, Brazilians, British, Chinese, Singaporeans, Spanish, South Africans, US-Americans*
few friends	*Indians*
if they do have friends then these are real, true friends	*Bulgarians*

Definition of Separation of Personality and Living Spheres

Germans make strict divisions between the various parts of their lives. They adjust their behaviour according to both the sphere in which they are dealing with another person as well as how close they are to that person.

Separation of the following spheres is fundamental:

- professional – private
- rational – emotional
- role – person
- formal – informal

A Brazilian has a German colleague. Since they often have dealings with each other, the Brazilian is taking great pains to get to know his German colleague better, however, he has the feeling that his colleague is not very friendly in return. One evening they happen to meet at the squash courts. All of a sudden the German seems completely different. He laughs, beckons his Brazilian colleague over and invites him to join him in a game. Afterwards they go out for a drink together. It is a very pleasant evening and the Brazilian thinks to himself, "Well, we've finally broken the ice. I always thought this German seemed nice and now I know it for sure." When he sees his German colleague in the office the next day he is pleased, approaches him with a smile and greets him with a joke about yesterday's squash game. The German, however, is like a different person: he is abrupt and doesn't respond to the joke but instead replies, "Sorry, I have a meeting in a few minutes, I'm in a hurry because I still have some preparation to do." He then turns away quickly, leaving the Brazilian rather taken aback. The German colleague hasn't just put on a suit for work, he's also buttoned up his personality, becoming just as uncommunicative as before their squash game. How could this be possible? Was he a different person yesterday?

A Spanish engineer has come to Germany for training in a particular production process which he is going to supervise upon his return to Spain. He is part of a working group with German colleagues who are all very friendly to him. One day, one of them invites him to his home for dinner. The Spaniard willingly accepts the invitation. He spends a pleasant evening with the colleague and his family, talking to both the colleague and his wife and playing with their children. The conversation covers many different topics, although work is not mentioned. They address each other with "Sie" (the polite form of "you"). The next morning they meet again in the office. To the astonishment of the Spaniard, his colleague, though as friendly as ever, stays on a purely professional level with him, without a single private word. The Spaniard wonders if the colleague's hospitality was genuine or whether he was only invited out of a feeling of duty because he is living alone in Germany.

Separation of Professional and Private

Germans work during work hours and "live" in their free time in the evenings, on the weekend and on holiday. In the workplace, work comes first and everything else takes a back seat. In private life, on the other hand, their time is taken up with relationships, friends, family, their own hobbies and interests. At work Germans are strictly business and task-oriented; in private life, they are focused on their personal relationships. At work, Germans are single-mindedly goal-oriented; in private, they want – and need – to relax. At work, Germans devote themselves to the content of the task at hand, in private life they indulge in very different activities and are thereby able to create a certain balance in life. To non-Germans it may seem as if they are dealing with two separate people with regards to their external appearance, their behaviour and their mood.

Colleagues are considered first and foremost as fellow workers, not as potential friends. Germans continue contacts with colleagues in their private lives on an evening off or at weekends only if that

141

person has already become a friend. Friendships within a circle of colleagues cannot be expected as a matter of course. Even business partners are not normally so close that they meet outside of work. More often than not, invitations from a business partner to his home are an exception and may remain very formal. These invitations usually only take place when there is a special occasion or for a particular reason.

In Prague, a Czech has quite a lot of German expats as colleagues. They get on quite well with one another and enjoy each other's company. Their relationships, however, have never extended beyond the office and seem to end with the end of the working day: they have never even gone out for a beer after work together. Everything runs perfectly until 5:00 p. m., If they happen to see him outside of work, they greet him, but no more, which the Czech man really regrets.

A Chinese hotel manager notices time and time again in his contact with his German business partners that it is difficult to be accepted into their group. Although he has been living in Germany for five years, he has only once been invited by a German to his home, and that was only because the German was the manager of the bank where he had received a loan for several million Euro. It's hard for him to understand that Germans never visit each other at home just to have a bit of a chat, without a specific reason. Instead, a formal invitation must nearly always be made. He believes that personal relationships like the ones in China just don't exist in Germany.

A businesswoman from Taiwan receives an invitation to dinner from her German tax consultant. She has known him for a long time now and has the feeling they are getting to be friends. Over dinner she begins, after a few polite but meaningless niceties, to talk about business matters. The tax consultant interrupts her, however, and asks her not to talk shop over a private, friendly meal. He invites her to save her questions for him for the next day in his office. For the Taiwanese businesswoman, this request is very unusual.

In Germany, friendships seldom develop from work, but are more likely to come about through sports clubs, through people sharing common interests, and through other private paths. The existence of a common interest is a good basis for a friendship.

As mentioned above, in business life work always comes first. One's private life is more or less put aside. For that reason, colleagues may know little about each other, apart from the more obvious personal characteristics (for example, marital status, hobbies and state of health). Only rarely are private matters and associated feelings spoken about – or asked about – in the workplace, and when they are it is only within a close and trusted relationship. Firstly, it is not the place for it; secondly, the drop in performance resulting from bringing personal matters into the workplace could, in a competitive environment, be used against the person. Even bosses take care not to get involved in the private lives of their employees. Such interference could be seen to have an ulterior motive.

A Polish man holds a managerial position in a German company. One of his employees is at home ill, so after a few days the Polish manager calls home to see how he is getting on. The employee does not sound as happy to hear from him as the Polish manager had expected; on the contrary, he sounds very distant and replies that he has already dutifully sent in his doctor's certificate to the personnel office. Thank you, goodbye. The Polish manager doesn't know what has happened: he wanted to be friendly, was sincerely interested in how the man was doing and is now being treated as though he is a spy and butting in where he's not welcome!

The rigid line between what is professional and private is clearly defined by norms (see *"Appreciation for Rules, Regulations and Structures"*) and emphasises the requirement that at work, one should concentrate on the matter at hand, but also that free time is there to be used for relaxation and regeneration and in order to be ready to work productively again. People are often very active and highly motivated in both spheres of life, which is why involvement in out-of-work activities is one of the criteria raised when it comes to personnel recruitment.

Because of the extreme separation of the two spheres of professional and private life, and because there is still inadequate childcare in Germany, it is especially difficult to combine raising a family with a career. In Germany, women in particular have to choose between having children and having a career. Because of the traditional allocation of gender roles and because much of the school system is organised on a half-day basis, women with children are seldom professionally active the entire day. They can often continue to work only part-time which does not help career advancement. Variations involving a mix of the two spheres meet with almost universal disapproval in the working world.

A Czech woman is managing a German firm in the Czech Republic. When her daughter gets sick and is in bed with a high fever she stays at home, in total for a week. During this time, she gets a call from the German owners asking where she is, as they need her at the firm. She answers that her child is ill and that she needs to look after her. To that the German owner replies, "For a whole week? What about having your husband stay at home for a while to relieve you – or perhaps you should make arrangements for a babysitter? You are after all the manager!" The Czech woman is perplexed; she has always stressed the fact that she has a child whom she may need to look after at home in the case of illness. She even arranged this with the owners beforehand. She cannot understand their critical tone.

Rational versus Emotional

Germans attempt to keep objective facts and feelings separate. Rationality is the order of the day, especially at work, where it is regarded as professional to remain objective (see *"Objectivism"*), and showing feelings may even be interpreted as a sign of weakness. Rationality is therefore the area of personality which is professionally active and constitutes the basis for objectivity and task-orientation. Emotionality on the other hand dominates private life, where it is important to be able to show sympathy and understanding for others as well as to be aware of one's own feelings and be able to express them.

Germans separate personal friendliness, which is reserved for the person behind the professional role, from professional criticism or objective performance appraisal, which refers strictly to the quality of work and the objective way a person fulfills their role. Thus, even otherwise friendly people can be harsh in their judgements and their demands on a professional basis.

Germans switch from being rational and objective to more emotional behaviour (as was shown in *"Rule-Oriented, Internalised Control"*) when they see a legitimate reason for doing so, for example, when something does not function according to the agreed-upon structure or strategy. In this case, Germans show their emotions first and foremost in a negative sense: they become openly annoyed, express their impatience and dissatisfaction, and even show anger and disappointment, though it stops short of insulting and abusive behaviour: the need to stay in a professional role ensures this.

Any failure at work or professional defeat greatly hurts and upsets Germans, but during working hours they force themselves to discipline their personal feelings and to live with the failure. Weaknesses can only be shown in small amounts, and the willingness to work things out must be placed before everything else. Persistence and the ability to continue functioning are seen as positive and productive. In crisis meetings, a practical approach of looking for objective causes is taken.

Germans have no trouble showing their emotions in other contexts, for example when they meet up with friends. Then even Italians or Czechs may find their emotional intensity *too* much, considering their public display of affection or soul-bearing too intimate and embarrassing. Another situation where Germans allow themselves to show their emotions is with humour: when jokes and silliness are called for, they can very easily amuse themselves in a boisterous fashion.

Role versus Person

Germans define their roles clearly and straightforwardly with respect to responsibility and authority. As long as the necessary structures are in place and are being used, it is expected that the roles will be fulfilled. Professionalism requires a complete knowledge of one's role, right down to the smallest details. A person is expected to stay properly "in role" whilst fulfilling the associated tasks and responsibilities. (see *"Rule-Oriented, Internalised Control"*).

A group of Czechs have been working for a German company in Prague for some time and have lived through many changes in the course of the company's development. Initially their company merged with another one, then the business operations of that company were sold and then there was another merger. That's the way the market works, the Czechs think. What totally astounds them is that their German boss tries to sell them every change with the words, "This is probably the best thing that could happen to us." Surely he is also suffering from the constant restructuring and insecurity? Why is he being so loyal? Why does he feel the need to support every one of these new decisions?

Professionalism means being correct and fair, remaining somewhat distant, having the relevant technical qualifications, and being committed to the job. The "real" person behind the role may be a lot more interesting and have many hidden facets. However, if that person wants to be recognised professionally, this personality must remain largely hidden. It is best to show only those aspects of personality that are clearly beneficial to the role and make the person look convincing in that role. To "slip out of the role" and show more personality than is strictly necessary to doing the job effectively is viewed negatively.

The individual hierarchical levels in an organization are distinguished from each other by the definition of their associated roles. Every level of the hierarchy has its own clearly defined responsibilities and people from higher levels tend not to get involved in the activities of lower levels. Employees from lower levels have some "room to move" within their defined roles, but make sure to do their work responsibly since their bosses have delegated certain parts of their authority to them and will only become involved in the case of conflict. The system of roles is confirmed again and again by certain rituals, for example, adhering strictly to the rules that define who has the right to sign which documents, who has the right to make which decisions, what the official channels of communication are and who bears ultimate responsibility.

Of particular importance to someone in a managerial position is the fact that any blurring of boundaries between his professional role and the other components of his personality could damage his authority as a manager. The German logic for this is as follows: a manager's job is to ensure that goals are reached by urging the employees to stick to their roles within the structure so that the common objective is served as effectively as possible. A more emotional relationship and the resulting closeness could lead to both the employees and the boss stepping out of role, and personal interests becoming inappropriately important (see "Regulation of Distance" in this chapter). As a result, the effectiveness of the system could be damaged by a conflict between objective, professional issues and emotional, personal interests. In the light of the important position of *objectivism* and all of the structures that support it, this is exactly what should *not* be allowed to happen. Accordingly, all managers take special care to concentrate on their role and to avoid close personal relationships with employees. Only then can a manager, in the event of a conflict, enforce the demands necessary to fulfill the objective task.

The manner in which people in a company interact with one another is largely determined in this way: even colleagues of equal rank deal with each other primarily through their roles.

146

An Indian manager has moved to Germany with his family. In India he is an important manager within the firm and he also holds a respected position in Germany, which should eventually enable him to take over the position of coordinator for the Indian subsidiary firm after becoming acquainted with the workings of the German headquarters. He is looking forward to his time in Germany, and during previous visits he has always been treated very courteously: he was picked up from the airport, the company had organised a special introductory program for him in the head office, and various German employees had taken time to entertain him and his delegation out of working hours. Since moving to Germany, however, he doesn't feel at all well treated by the company, and he is bitterly disappointed. Nobody has made him feel particularly welcome, nobody has been looking after his family, and nobody makes time for him. They have merely found him an apartment, informed him of the address, left him the key, welcomed him in the office where he was to work, introduced him to the most important men and women in his department and suggested that the international personnel department could help him with any general questions. He is told that if he has any questions about his work he could ask the colleagues in his local office, which turns out to be true. Nevertheless, from his point of view, he feels totally "abandoned." Everybody is friendly, but no-one is really looking after him and his family.

The key to understanding this scenario lies in the separation of living spheres in Germany: the Indian manager is no longer a guest, but now more or less a "normal" colleague with a clearly defined role, who is there to work and whose private life is simply that: his own private affair.

Formal versus Informal

The Germans also make a distinction between formal and informal situations. Important matters which arise during the normal working day are dealt with through formal channels, in official meetings. This is the time and place for expressing opinions and getting involved in the decision-making process because this is where the discussions and agreements take place. In this context the points of discussion are tangible, comprehensible and accessible to all. Whatever Germans organise under the conceptual heading of *"Appreciation for Rules, Regulations and Structures"* has a real significance for them at work, which is why so many formal discussions and meetings are held in Germany. That is the time and place to share information, express opinions and make joint decisions. This can mean a repetition of content because important matters are repeatedly discussed within the respective framework and what has already been said informally is now said again formally. Only then does it become valid and only then can the speaker be sure that it will not be ignored. Even team discussions are officially organised and it is not uncommon for someone to take detailed minutes. Whoever has anything to say must speak up now and not later because this is when and where decisions take place: afterwards it will be too late. (see *"Time Planning"*).

Low-context, step-by-step time planning and the preference for formal structures are closely related to each other: Germans first register things when they are on an agenda and when they can formally concentrate on them.

The German-Polish negotiations are making little progress and the general mood is grim. The interpreter explains that one reason for this is that, "The Germans insist that they can't possibly proceed without several documents and pieces of information which, according to the minutes, they should have received beforehand. However, the Poles say they've already either said or given everything necessary to the Germans; but at different points in time and totally unsystematically, sometimes here, sometimes there; sometimes one of them said something and sometimes someone else said something different; sometimes they addressed it to one German and then sometimes to another. The Germans appear to have forgotten or never registered this informally channelled information, and in fact for weeks have been complaining that this information and these documents are lacking. They insist on working through the agenda in the order that the points are listed and consider the Poles unprofessional. The Poles are annoyed that they are supposed to compile everything and pass it on yet again and consider the Germans to be pedantic and authoritarian."

In order to document the course of many events, formal information channels such as mailing lists, newsletters and reporting systems are often set up. These channels are taken seriously, and the important information necessary for work progress *is really* transferred in this way. There are separate discussion and conference rooms for meetings. The flow of information through the correct channels should ensure that all meeting participants are equally up-to-date on the situation so that they can, if necessary, be involved in the problem-solving process. In this way everyone can feel included in the same, fair manner; they can express their opinions and participate actively in decision-making.

If there is something to talk about or arrange, then Germans contact each other through the official, formal channels in accordance with their respective roles. Usually no additional mediation is required, and it is not necessary for the individuals to know each other beforehand.

A Czech marketing manager for a small business subsidiary in the Czech Republic is on a short visit to the headquarters of his company in Germany. It is absolutely imperative that he obtains some particular information from the marketing department in Germany, so he contacts someone in the marketing department and asks for the information to be ready by 12 o'clock because he then has to return to the Czech Republic. The German actually carries out his request, much to the surprise of the Czech, who is suitably impressed! The German did this for him even though he didn't know him personally.

Since there is such a strong emphasis on formal structures in Germany, German hierarchies are often very clearly visible down to the last detail. Furthermore, it is openly acknowledged that the manager of one level should first reach an agreement with those of a higher level before something new can be implemented. This behaviour is not a sign of timidity, nor does it show a submissive dependence on authority; it is simply observing the official channels.

The following can be said regarding informal structures, which of course also exist in Germany:

1. At work, informal relationships should not replace formal ones! Formal relationships take precedence over informal relationships and determine the way daily work is conducted.

2. Informal relationships, on the other hand, reflect a relationship based on liking someone. This is why Germans, striving to be correct, try *not* to give these relationships a special status in their work dealings and instead attempt to remain strictly objective. They do not want to be accused of nepotism. They therefore follow the formal structures to the letter, fully in accordance with any regulations that may exist, despite the presence of any informal relationships.

3. Informal connections may be used officially when the formal structures themselves have become a barrier, as happens in some large companies. In this case, the informal structures have a simplifying and compensatory effect which makes them acceptable.

4. The use of connections in Germany is limited to actual personal acquaintances: mediation or some arrangement through a third party is not acceptable. It is also necessary to have a high degree of trust. (compare with *"Separation of Living Spheres: friendship"*).

5. Furthermore, the existing network of connections and relationships tends to be relatively small and restricted. There are very few instances in which acquaintances and personal connections can help someone to pursue an interest. Normally, the official, formal route is the only one to follow.

6. Giving presents of any kind may be seen as bribery and corruption.

7. Informal relationships are more often used in "office politics," for instance, during power struggles. Because of this, personal connections often have the reputation of being a way to scheme sneakily in business. Such "office politics" seldom impact on the working lives of normal employees.

Self-Assurance in One's Role

To many other cultures, Germans appear to be very self-assured, or to put it in a less complimentary way, arrogant. Being self-assured is usually the correct interpretation, at least of Germans in their professional roles. Germans feel themselves to be specialists in their fields, and they certainly have that image in their company or they would not have been entrusted with their responsibilities. They thus remain free of major doubts about their professional abilities. Their stance is based on this confidence, and they often state their opinion whether or not it has been called for. Through long-winded statements or pedantic attention to detail, they create at least the impression of being an expert. They use the typically direct German style of communication: they contradict, they correct, are opinionated and argumentative. This is all the more true when Germans have economic advantage on their side during a negotiation.

Nevertheless – believe it or not – this aspect of German behaviour should not be equated with national pride! There is another side to the coin: German insecurity. It remains hidden as long as the contact is of a professional nature and everyone stays in their professional roles. It is in their relationships with many of their European neighbours that these diverse insecurities catch up with many Germans, and the more conscientious and correct a person is, the worse it is. History lies heavy on Germans, and a positive national consciousness can be found only in the guise of pride in business achievements, never as an intact national identity. However, the separation of professional and private spheres enables a retreat into "roles" thus preventing both Germans and non-Germans from being confronted with this insecure side. Germans discuss this aspect of their identity only amongst themselves (as well as in intercultural training in which they prepare to live in a culture that suffered under Germans in the past). Some critical fellow citizens are of the opinion that German business achievements are, in fact, attempts at compensation, sometimes very consciously and at other times unconsciously.

Regulation of Distance

Distance also plays a distinctive role in German social contact. One and the same person may show varying behaviour in interactions depending on whether the other person is a stranger, a colleague, an acquaintance or a close friend. The development of a friendship is a pleasant exception. As a general rule, it can be said that:

a) Distanced and formal contact is the first step.

b) This initial distance and objectivity give way to increasing emotionality, sincerity and person-orientation.

c) Friendship and intimacy is a matter of the heart and is not determined by logic and the advantages the friendship could bring.

d) There is little interest in continually meeting new people, therefore many contact possibilities are not taken advantage of and active attempts to make contact or uninvited interference may easily be considered pushy. Instead, keeping your distance and being reserved are perceived as polite, and it has to be accepted that first contacts may lead nowhere. Customers, although treated in a friendly and polite manner, are also kept at a distance.

e) Differentiation of relationships according to social distance is perfectly illustrated by the distinct informal and formal forms of address ('Du' and 'Sie').

Friendship progresses step by step: first neutral behaviour, progressing cautiously to increasing emotional openness, then friendliness and finally to sincere warmth. This progression takes, depending upon the age and willingness of those involved, anything from a few weeks to years.

The *social-emotional* behavioural steps that Germans take in approaching and getting to know someone can be portrayed by a series of *stages*.

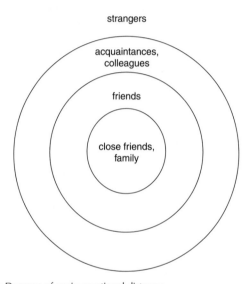

Figure 3: Degrees of socio-emotional distance.

Relationships with Strangers

Germans usually avoid contact with strangers. There has to be a reason to speak to someone or it may well be interpreted as being impolite or pushy, and the desire to meet new people is often absent. If social contact is initiated, Germans usually start off by acting in a reserved and neutral manner. They may interact on a purely objective level and slip into a comfortable role, such as their professional one. This is often interpreted as being cold, reserved or ill-humoured, especially as Germans are not seen as big smilers. The form of address is definitely the formal "Sie."

A French manager hates travelling in the German underground train system because of the deathly quiet: the passengers don't talk to one another. If acquaintances do meet they speak in hushed tones, as if they don't want to disturb the silence of the others. He has the feeling that in the German underground there must be some rule, similar to in the library, that everyone has to be quiet.

An Indonesian is living in an apartment house in Germany. Each day five people from the building leave for the local train station. They usually leave the building almost simultaneously, greet each other, walk to the station and wait for one or two minutes in silence, making no effort to engage each other in conversation.

Two Germans share a table in the cafeteria. A Mexican sits down next to them. He greets them. They return the greeting curtly and then carry on their conversation. Time and time again he attempts to enter into the conversation, but they appear to want to ignore him, answering him as briefly as possible before continuing their own conversation. The Mexican is very disappointed: he would have enjoyed a lunchtime chat!

An American is distressed that it is so difficult to come into closer contact with his German colleagues. He is greeted politely, he is spoken to as much as it is necessary for work purposes, but there is no simple "chatting." Moreover, he receives no social invitations. No-one shows any interest in him or wants to question him about his personal life above and beyond professional co-operation. The American is irritated. This is not how he'd imagined settling in Germany would be like. He also finds this type of behaviour to be very rude.

Appropriate subjects for initiating social contact should be factual and objective, not anything concerning personal or family matters *(see "Objectivism")*. From the German perspective this does not indicate indifference towards the feelings of a person, but reflects the gradual development and construction of a personal relationship.

A French employee finds it difficult to make friends with Germans. His colleagues already know each other and discuss their hobbies, house construction, investments, experiences with their children and so forth. The Frenchman is simply not an insider and cannot contribute to these discussions. If he does make a personal remark such as that his sister is getting married or that his mother is celebrating her 60th birthday, then his German colleagues look blankly and say, "Oh yes?" He feels that Germans need more time than other people before they feel comfortable enough and have sufficient trust in a person to be able to discuss personal matters.

Making contact with Germans often relies on the initiative of the foreigner. Some (polite) Germans do not want to intrude, others simply do not know what to say. Of course, both of these problems do not exist when dealing with existing acquaintances.

An American has just recently arrived in Germany and wonders time and again about her German colleagues. Whenever she is in the coffee break room her colleagues will not speak to her until she herself says something. Whenever she wants to talk to someone she has to initiate the conversation. Whenever the Germans are talking among themselves they include her in the conversation only after she has said something on the subject in question. But even then, she often still finds it very difficult because Germans frequently discuss politics, a subject which she knows little about. However, when another German enters the room, he or she is immediately included in the discussion. She finds such behaviour strange, and it upsets her greatly as she had hoped to make new friends in Germany.

Relationships with Acquaintances and Colleagues

The characteristic German reserve is currently on the wane. German behaviour in encounters with others is changing to become generally more friendly and obliging. *Acquaintances* still keep their distance and do not show any deeper feelings. Germans still fill their respective social and professional roles perfectly and only instigate closer, private contact with people they really like. Accordingly, official obligations out of office hours are still commonly viewed as sacrificing one's free-time. In the office, functional and unemotional interaction is still the norm.

Despite the fact that in younger and more "laid-back" teams the familiar form of address ("Du") may be predominant, the polite form of address ("Sie") is still widely used, especially where there is an age difference between the people involved. Here the use of formality demonstrates both self-respect and respect for the other person, and it unveils the character of the relationship: everybody stays within their commonly accepted role and behaves in a correct, albeit polite and friendly fashion. Customers are also treated politely but distantly.

In principle, this way of interacting with one another makes it possible to work well together even with less-liked colleagues. At the same time, this formal level of interaction serves as a starting point for finding out whether somebody seems interesting on a personal level, because of the hints of what he or she might do, know or think.

Favourite topics to talk about apart from work-related matters often include health and illness, travelling and hobbies.

An Indian greatly enjoys the coffee breaks with her German colleagues: they can talk forever about various illnesses. Everybody seems to be suffering from something and everything gets discussed in great detail.

Questions concerning the private life of colleagues have to be asked prudently and this is even more so when talking to a boss.

Having recently graduated from the university, a young North American is working as an administrative officer. To have a form signed, he goes to the office of the head of department and finds him in the anteroom talking to his secretary. Whilst he is there the head of department asks him where he is from, how he likes Germany, how long he will stay and what his future plans are. The American enjoys the conversation and decides to ask his superior if he would like to go to a party with him. The head of department answers that he won't be able to come because he has to drive to Munich. When the American employee asks him what he will be doing in Munich, the head of department ends the conversation by curtly replying, "It's a private matter." This offends and hurts the American's feelings. His superior had obviously enjoyed talking to him a minute ago, he had even asked him personal questions, which seemed to make it clear that he wanted to talk more with him. Why did he suddenly become so cold and stand-offish?

The distance between superiors and subordinates can usually be compared to the distance between acquaintances. In this context, the use of the polite form of address ("Sie") takes on a significant meaning: it ensures that the focus lies on the job and the task at hand because private and professional spheres should not be mingled. If they were to come closer together, the emotional distance would decrease and make the execution of leadership more difficult. This is because friendship (or warm-heartedness) belongs to the private sphere and brings with it the obligation to take personal and emotional matters into account. This would limit the boss's ability to remain objective and demand the absolute optimum from his employees. It could also encourage the employees to drop the demands of their roles and follow their momentary feelings.

An Englishman is the head engineer for a large construction company in Germany. Since this company does the plans and cost calculations for large projects like freeway-overpasses, he has a great deal of responsibility. As engineering mistakes can result in very serious damage, he is very concerned and careful that no false calculations from within his department reach sub-contracted construction companies. He has a good working relationship with all of his employees, and in England he is used to addressing his employees by their first-names. Thus, everyone in his department uses the familiar form of addressing each other ("Du"), even with him. Now, one of his engineers has made a very grave error. As soon as the English head-engineer becomes aware of it he goes directly to this employee to "have a few words" with him. The German employee listens to him and then says: "Calm down, Clive, don't get all worked up. Let's just go out for a beer and forget about it."

An Indian living in Germany works as a software developer. Because of an impending delivery date, all of the developers are very concerned because the software hasn't been completely tested. During a meeting the Indian and his colleagues have with their boss, it comes to light that a particular machine is needed to perform the necessary tests. This machine is in another city so they'll have to take a business trip there. The Indian is surprised by the situation that one of his colleagues is thrown into. When this colleague says he can only stay on the business trip for a few days because his wife is at home with a small baby and needs him, their boss promptly replies, "We can't take that into consideration. Maybe you'll have to stay there for two or three weeks. I can't promise you that it will only take one or two days. You're here to work! I don't care how you organise it but you have a job to do. You may have to work Saturdays and Sundays as well. And there's nothing more to discuss." Since the Indian is single this is no problem for him. Besides that, he'll enjoy being away on business for a few days. But his poor German colleague! He can understand his dilemma. How can their boss be so heartless? Why doesn't he take the personal issues of his employee into consideration? Why does he act so harshly?

Stories like this one are part of the reality of working life for many Germans in higher positions. Of course, each scenario is different and may have more or less compromise. This particular one, however, clearly demonstrates the main points: the boss's goal is to make sure the job gets done successfully and he has little consideration for his employees.

The relationship between neighbours is usually on a similar level to that between colleagues and acquaintances: neighbours know each other by sight, greet each other and exchange a few neutral words, but there is rarely more contact than this.

An Indian has been living with his family in Germany for three years. They live in an apartment building. He now knows the apartment-house manager, a couple (the man is Italian, his wife German), all of the Brazilian and American tenants, but he still hasn't met a single one of the German families, although they see each other every day. The Indian has only a very small circle of German friends. It took him a very long time to get used to this.

Social Contact between Good Acquaintances and Friends

Once you have been accepted into a circle of German friends or have at least one German friend, you will notice that you are treated significantly differently – namely, better. It can be described in the following manner:

Individuals make a conscious choice about who they want to be friends with. These are, without exception, people they get along with well and like a lot. Now the familiar form of addressing each other on a first-name basis is used ("Du"). Good acquaintances progressively share more of their personality with one another; in other words they speak more openly about their attitudes, opinions and problems. They make appointments to meet each other in their free time. At this stage of a relationship inviting each other over, nurturing the relationship, being willing to help each other out, sharing emotions as well as giving gifts on special occasions such as birthdays comes to be the norm. Physical contact is completely normal and emphasises the close bond. Once a trusting relationship has been built up, loyalty and help in the face of problems is expected. Of course, visits occur in the home, not somewhere neutral as is the case with more distant relationships.

The next stage in a relationship is friendship. This is where friends can be completely open and share all of their feelings, worries and joys. Friendships are bound by deep feelings and are long lasting. A friendship is emotionally fuelled and exists only because of mutual affection. It is very hurtful if someone tries to gain something through a friendship (for example, material gain, connections, status, and so on). The person involved will feel very used.

Similar ways of looking at the world, shared experiences, common interests and hobbies are some of the most important elements that foster friendship. For this reason, participating in one or more free-time activities or clubs can be an enormous aid to finding new friends. When common interests exist, it is easier to jump over the stage of being an "unknown" and even to leave behind the stage of "acquaintance" more quickly to reach friendship.

An Indian has been living in Germany for three years. Just by chance he sees a message on the bulletin board in the cafeteria that says that the Hiking Club is now meeting again regularly, and that next weekend they are planning an excursion. Since he doesn't want to spend the whole weekend alone he thinks it might be a good idea to give them a call. Of course, he is more than welcome to participate, he is told on the telephone. The young Indian thus goes on the first hike of his life. Everyone is nice and friendly and is in a good mood, and it seems they are happy that he is having a good time. He is asked if he wants to come along again next week, and if so, he will need more appropriate clothing. He has received an invitation! It also turns out that someone has an anorak for him and someone else has some hiking boots that he can have. He feels almost smothered in friendship. In the meantime he is perfectly equipped with everything he needs, he is doing something with a group of people every weekend, and during the week he is constantly being invited to get together, since there are photos to be looked at or the next hike needs to be planned or someone just wants to go out with "the group." Now he has made some real friends who are even willing to help him with his integration and adaptation problems. They all really like each other!

Oscillating between the Two Poles

Generally speaking, *"The Separation of Personality and Living Spheres"* means that the more rigidly people stay within their defined and boundaried spheres, the greater the distance between them. Boundaries become blurred amongst friends; amongst acquaintances they are clearer. Germans move between these ways of operating.

The starting point in professional contexts is this: colleagues meet each other at work on a professional level (not on a private level), stress their rationality (not their emotionality), and stay properly within their roles (without a personal "flavour") within the formal structures of their company.

In the process of getting to know one another, maybe even of becoming friends, colleagues subtly start changing their roles to become acquaintances or friends and their distance decreases. Their contact becomes more private, emotionality is given more room, the other person's personality becomes visible in all of its facets, and informal settings and structures become established. Good friends eventually reach the level on which words like "private," "emotional," "person" and "informal" really come to life.

Nevertheless, the focus in a relationship may be subject to continual change.

- When friends meet at work they concentrate on the job, and when they meet privately, they concentrate on the personal matters.
- A very "correct" person may even fall back to formally addressing the friend with "Sie," just to show how seriously they both take their professional roles, and that they are not, under any circumstances, going to allow their relationship to lead to nepotism.
- During normal working hours it is normal to stay "in role," but at birthday parties (during working hours) or while on a company excursion "real" personalities become more obvious, and it is possible to pay attention to nurturing relationships.
- Whenever matters of great importance are discussed, it is normal for all involved to clearly differentiate between what their rational, sensible side thinks of the problem as opposed to their emotional and intuitive side. These two sides have to be weighed against each other in order for a decision to be made.
- Even among close friends some formality may remain (for example, polite gestures, polite formal words) as a way of showing respect for one another.

The German ability to completely switch from one sphere to another is distinctive and can be annoying.

When an Indian expatriate gets to the office he finds out that yesterday their team-leader, who has been fighting cancer for some time now, has died. As the work day begins all of his colleagues are sitting around the office speaking about how sad they are about his death. He was very well liked and will be missed. After a while someone says, "Oh well, none of this is going to change the situation. We can't do anything about it. Let's get to work, our project is due the day after tomorrow," at which point everyone actually gets up from the group and goes back to work. From this moment on it seems to the Indian that everything is back to normal. Only now he is so upset about this tragic death that he cannot concentrate on his work. It seems however, that he is the only one who feels this way.

While this example may support the stereotype of the heartless German, it is also true that Germans can be very affectionate and nice.

As hosts, they can be very friendly, extremely positive, polite, obliging and very attentive. As friends they are very appreciative and sincere. They can live out this side of their life to the full when they, so to speak, give it their full concentration. A woman from Slovakia expresses it as follows: "We Slovakians are polite and considerate hosts. But we are never as polite and as considerate as the Germans once they have decided to taken it upon themselves to be hosts."

The Pros and Cons of the Culture Standard "Separation of Personality and Living Spheres"

The advantage of this culture standard lies in the fact that it increases effectiveness at work. Work-related tasks, which are objective and rational, and involve other people with whom there are few social obligations, can be carried out in a concentrated manner. The emotional and social deprivations that may result from this culture standard for individuals are well compensated for in the private sphere by their family and friends.

A major disadvantage of this standard has already been discussed: this system is hard on people who have no possibility for compensation, that is, who have no family "nest" to which they can retreat in order to renew their energy.

There is another danger that occurs when the life-spheres are separated: if the differentiation is too extreme, the authenticity or integrity of the person as a rounded whole can be endangered. The discrepancies in German behaviour and compartmentalisation of their lives often make them seem fake or even schizophrenic to foreigners. Even Germans themselves notice that they have a certain one-sidedness, and that some of their peers seem to lack integrated personalities.

When formal structures and roles are particularly emphasised, another important disadvantage occurs: because everyone is so concentrated on their goals, guidelines and tasks, they fail to consider how their job interfaces and overlaps with the work of their colleagues. How can they, since there is no real contact between them? As a result, a precious resource of information goes completely untapped. The formal channels of communication and information flow are often not sophisticated enough to make up for the ensuing information deficit.

Recommendations

Suggestions for non-Germans Working with Germans:

- You are mistaken if you think Germans are the "cold robots" you often encounter in the work force. Germans are also capable of falling in love with one another, devotedly raising their children, being true friends to each other, engaging themselves socially and being involved in charitable or voluntary organisations. It is just that their hearts are reserved for their loved ones, and when they are at work they "put their noses to the grindstone" as if they have to earn this free time.

- If Germans seem cold to you, you should not assume that you are personally at fault. More likely than not they just want to act "correctly" and in context, whether that is being responsible at work, being task and goal oriented (rational), taking their job seriously (role) and working within structures (formalities).

- Be prepared to invest a lot of time into developing friendships with Germans. They need time to warm to others. The length of time it takes has nothing to do with you. And in the meantime, be careful about asking personal questions.

- Take the initiative to get to know people, especially when you are living in Germany. Germans don't mean to be unfriendly, but your colleagues already belong to a circle of friends and acquaintances and are therefore less interested in making new friends than you may be. Join some sort of a group or a club in your free-time. You will find the acceptance level to be much higher here.

- If you are organising some sort of an event (for example, with other people from your home country), expressly invite your German colleagues to participate as well. This is a good way to break the ice and open the doors to new friendships. Any German who comes will be doing so in their free time, and this fact alone means that they will be feeling more open towards you.

- Make it a habit to share anything that you feel is important at the appointed formal time (for example, at meetings). It is also best to wait until it is your turn and to make sure that your points of interest are already on the agenda. This will involve planning ahead. In this way you will be heard and taken seriously – information that is informally said may get lost! This is because Germans may not recognise this to be your opinion and contribution to the conversation or to the topic at hand (see *"Low Context"*).

Recommendations for Germans Working with non-Germans

- Be friendly and polite, not just correct!
- Show both sides of your personality by talking about yourself and revealing different aspects of your personality. This is the best way to create the necessary basis for forming a good working relationship and eventually friendships with many foreigners.
- Be attentive towards the colleagues you directly work with. Take note of personal information you learn about your colleagues, and try to show more interest in their lives than you would in Germany. When they show interest in you, allow yourself to enjoy the experience of making new friends.
- Help others, especially when you are asked, even in private matters.
- Try to be less remote, more easy-going, more personal. No matter how well you do your job, you will not impress anyone unless you can convince them that you are also a nice person. This can be reinforced by a kind gesture, a comment or a bit of humour – whatever fits your personality.
- Learn to work with informal structures. The German tendency to hold formal meetings is seen by many foreigners as being a cumbersome and complicated method of sharing information, and for many it seems overly authoritarian.
- Don't force yourself into an informal group. Give yourself and others time! Show that you're helpful and interested.
- Accept that the walls separating the different areas of your life will eventually get thinner, as keeping them in place will demand too much energy. It is more important to decide which parts of yourself and your life are truly private and keep the wall intact around them. In other areas you can let the drawbridge down a bit so that others can pass over. Being human and not being afraid to show weaknesses and vulnerability can make you more likeable, expressing emotions also makes you more human, a private life is vital for happiness, and informality can help unite people and encourage trust and agreement.
- Don't be mistaken in thinking that foreigners think Germans are hard workers. For those foreigners living in Germany, this is def-

initely not the case! The fact that Germans adhere strictly to their short (albeit intense) working hours and are very serious about having free-time ("hard work and hard play") often makes Germans appear cold, unemotional and lazy to foreigners.

Historical Background

How can the *"Separation of Personality- and Life Spheres"* be explained? It is a typically German characteristic, which along with objectivity and task focus exists throughout Western cultures, but is particularly well-developed in Germany, with many diverse aspects. Particular periods played a special role in these developments.

In the centuries of German *territorial fragmentation,* restrictions and confinement were everyday experiences. Boundaries of daily reality increasingly became "boundaries of the mind" as well. By the middle of the 18th century, there were approximately 1600 different territories on German soil, and even at the beginning of the 19th century some 1000 still existed, the boundaries of which could not be easily crossed. "They formed independent legal entities, were often also boundaries of religion and modelled people's experiences in different but fundamental ways. Central decisions in an individual's life depended on the local rules and customs: for example, the right to get married, the right to set up a business, professional and feudal ties, customs regarding law of inheritance, the education system and social welfare" (Althaus et al. 1992a, p. 46). The separation of internal (personal) and external (impersonal) areas became especially distinctive: people led a confined life-style in a small circle of close friends.

Such privacy also provided important protection against falling into the clutches of the reigning absolute ruler. A separation of "external" and "internal" life, accompanied by a separation of the accompanying personality spheres (for example, duty, obedience and social role on the one hand, rich inner life, personal development, and personality on the other), as well as clear differentiation between strangers and friends was a natural reaction to the political circumstances:

– The reforms of the Enlightenment brought with them a "nationalisation" of life everywhere. People were happy to accept the care provided by an authoritative welfare-state but not necessarily its increasing tendency to rule private life. This gave rise to "the desire for demarcation, for protection of the private sphere . . . (and) for repulsion of state intervention" (Althaus et a. 1992c, p. 96). Whilst the citizens in many other European states had already reached the pinnacle of their power and influence and were now shaping public life, the Restoration in Germany abruptly stopped all developments in this direction. "The result was increased polarisation in which the family, on the one hand, became a haven of trust, compassion, reliability and closeness, and civil society and the state, on the other hand, became a place for matter-of-fact relations in which power and formal hierarchy regulated mutual relations. (. . .) A sort of double standard established itself (. . .). In the face of the objective and hierarchical relations in the public sphere, idealisation of the private sphere, comprising family and friendship ties . . . came into being" (Kalberg 1988, p. 13 f.). "True German life takes place in the innermost realms (. . .). Here the German is in his element, here his being blossoms and we owe German philosophy, German literature, German music and art, German seriousness to this retreat into inwardness" (Sana 1986, p. 97). The retreat of the over-controlled citizens into privacy reached its peak during the Biedermeier period and the Restoration, and its ideological companion was German idealism and romanticism: in private life the citizen refreshes heart, mind and soul (Kalberg 1988; Münch 1993; Sauzay 1986). An intense secular inwardness was cultivated, and between 1750 and 1850 German intellectual life and art flourished and the phenomena of the Enlightenment were deeply embedded in the classical poetry and idealistic philosophy of Germany in this period (Kindermann). Especially at a time when Germany was unable to assert itself politically or militarily on the European stage and when the princes ruled locally, a compensatory counter-movement developed which gave prominence to the inner worth of the German character (Nuss 1992).

– When the National Assembly in St. Paul's Church in Frankfurt failed in its efforts to bring about reforms in 1848, this development was furthered once again, and the retreat into privacy became an expression of resignation and in some states also protection against persecution. Sections of the middle-class remained without lasting political influence until the Weimar Republic, and there was, for a long time, no movement against this.

The already thriving industrialisation process brought about a similar development within the lower classes of society: extended families were split up, the father was no longer at home, and later still, not even the mother or children were at home. The severity and speed of this radical change, which went totally against the tradition of the territorial family, delivered a shock to the social fabric. The counter-reaction led once again to retreat into privacy and a personal life (Molz 1994).

The ideological atmosphere further intensified the trend.

– In around 1800 family life based on expression of feelings, emotional solidarity and a personal parent-child relationship emerged throughout Europe. In Germany this refinement of subjectivity and emotionalism was felt mainly in the personal, inner sphere, not in the political and social sphere. Family, literature, nature, friendship – such experiences determined personal fulfillment, strengthening the power of the private sphere even more. It was at this time that gender roles began to polarise, especially in German states, because of the lack of a vocal citizenry (Bausinger 2000).

– The German ideal of friendship which developed during the periods of Romanticism and Idealism had a profound effect on sections of society. It consisted of a "very high degree of intimacy, feeling and warmth" (Kalberg 1988, p. 13) as well as life-long mutual obligation, and this was vital, as in the enlightened, authoritarian small states, the intellectuals could only escape their isolation through having true and loyal friends. Friendships enabled the lower classes to re-establish a large substitute family. In an era of massive social and economic change accompanied by the "dissolution of the old social orders and ties" (Althaus et al. 1992, p. 102), the ideal of friendship promised stability and direction.

Group activities and festivals provided an opportunity for "privacy in public"; a chance to create a harmonious, community spirit amongst like-minded people, and served the third sphere which is somewhere between family life and public life (Althaus et al. 1992c; Kalberg 1988; Bausinger 2000). This communal activity allowed the representation of diverse interests and put official duties in the areas of education, public issues and politics under private control. "In ever-renewed waves new social groups developed this convivial and organisational form to pursue their interests and needs" (Althaus et al. 1992c, p. 103). The political effect of these developments could not be denied and was by no means neutral, and as a result heavy restrictions were imposed.

This entire development would probably not have been so extreme if *Protestantism* had not delivered the supportive theology for it: Luther made a distinction between "private and religious inwardness" and "public world" or "social formalities" (Münch 1993; Nipperdey 1991). He then developed the doctrine of the two realms:

a) *Inwardness* relates to the morality of the heart as expressed in the "Sermon on the Mount" in the New Testament (Troeltsch 1925). This relates to a feeling, belief and trust in God and is primarily defined in a religious manner. Personal fulfillment is attained by dedication to God.

b) *The public world or formalities* relates to secular life, which came about because of the Original Sin (Troeltsch 1925), and is regulated through work-related norms and the laws and regulations of the land. According to Luther's doctrine, policy-making is left to the sovereign ruler. The subject must obey that ruler except for instructions which contravene the commandments of God – in which case one can point this out or flee but not express active resistance (see *"Rule-Oriented, Internalised Control"*). A person has to conduct themselves with regard for the social fabric.

The two spheres are consequently strictly separate from one another: fundamental belief does not have to be expressed through actions if trust in God is preserved; whereas social action means playing a role, and personal identity does not need to contribute to this and be completely revealed (Münch 1993). This means that someone can be a completely different person inside, where there is freedom from the formalities of life, the battles, ambition and the pursuit of interests. "Inwardness and Christian belief stand above the hustle and bustle of the world, institutions, the law, activities" (Nipperdey 1991, p. 43). As we have seen, this Lutheran inwardness later becomes a personality ideal.

The last wave strengthening the phenomenon *"Separation of Personality and Living Spheres"* was the total collapse at the end of the Third Reich. The moral condemnation (both from within and outside of Germany) of all political and public life had the same effect once more: as an expression of humiliation and an attempt to cope with events, there was an aversion to everything public and a retreat into the security of privacy and small groups and familiar connections. (Kalberg 1988; Klages 1987).

Above all, Germany's defeat in two World Wars as well as its previous backwardness in the era of small territorial states gave rise to its much-discussed negative self-image. Nevertheless, Germans are often perceived as being arrogant and extremely self-assured. The explanation for this contradiction is as follows: self-assuredness is part of acting out the *role* and is not generally present, especially within the national identity. If the literature (cultural and historical) refers to a positive German self-esteem at all, it is in terms of this ambivalence. Admittedly, economic prosperity, global respect based on the political and economic reconstruction and the largely normal existence as a prosperous industrial state have formed the positive lifestyle of modern Germany. The question regarding German identity, however, still causes embarrassment. Assertive behaviour and impressive display can be used to mask this (Krockow 1989), and pride in a prospering economy and the respective achievements tend to replace national pride. "That is the reason for the inner anxiety, which hides behind their superficial self-satisfaction and occasional boasting"(Sana 1994, p. 178).

■ Low Context: the German Style of Communication

How Germans are perceived by other cultures	
direct, clear, honest, sincere, undiplomatic, unfriendly	*Australians, Brazilians, British, Bulgarians, Chinese, Indians, Japanese, Koreans, Mexicans, Spaniards, Turks, Hungarians, US-Americans*
enjoy discussions, argue at meetings, contradict, interrupt if they have an objection	*Brazilians, Finns, Japanese, Koreans, Spaniards*
criticise others very directly	*Spaniards*
insensitive, tough	*Brazilians*
help is not offered, one must ask	*Brazilians, Chinese, British, Indians, Swedes, Spaniards, Turks*
answer only what has been asked	*Brazilians*
are true to their word, do what they say they are going to do	*Brazilians Indians, Spaniards*
100% yes or 100% no – no grey zones (like yes, but . . .)	*Indians, Japanese*
predictable, calculable, candid	*Chinese, Czechs*
humourless, not sarcastic, take everything literally, do not make fun of themselves	*British, Koreans, Spaniards, Czechs, Hungarians*
write everything down, more paper than verbal communication	*Indians, Poles, Spaniards*
not talkative, often silent (for example, at meals)	*Brazilians, Spaniards, US-Americans*

The term "context" describes the phenomenon that occurs when not all of the information that we need to understand a situation is vocalised, so that something remains unspoken. How much information is explicitly and clearly expressed compared with the complete version varies depending upon the situation. If a large portion of the message remains unspoken, it is considered to have a "high-context," whereas if most of the message is verbally formulated and does not need additional interpretation, the amount of context necessary to understand it is low, and it is termed "low-context."

Definition of "Low Context"

The German communication style is famous for being very explicit and direct. Germans formulate what is important to them fully and verbally, making the content clear and unambiguous. The characteristic elements of this style of communication are:

1. The question *what* is in the foreground, while the *how* remains in the background. The focus is on objectivity: on the task level. For Germans the content of *what* is said is important and not *how* it is said.
2. Germans speak in a very frank, sometimes undiplomatic way without trying to cover anything up. They are very honest and sincere, and they say whatever they have to say exactly as they see it. They clearly express their opinions and come to the point without digressing.
3. They tend not to take personal sensibilities into consideration, and can therefore make unintentionally hurtful statements. Germans have a difficult time talking themselves out of these situations as they are bad liars, and consider honesty to be the fundamental basis of a trusting relationship.
4. This style leaves little "room to move" in a communicative sense. Germans want to express themselves precisely and clearly when they speak, in a manner that cannot be misunderstood: they mean what they say, and they say what they mean. In order to understand the message fully, the listener only needs a very small amount of supplementary information. It is expected that people will spell out exactly what they want, as allusions and hints will not be understood.

5. On the other hand, Germans only tend to understand *exactly* what has been said. It does not occur to them that this may only be part of the message, and that they need to take note of other information or signals to receive the full message. They hear the spoken words, they take it for granted that what is said is exactly what is meant, and they do not see the necessity for further decoding or interpretation.

6. Because Germans use *time planning* and prefer *formal structures* as the forum for sharing information, it does not occur to them that someone may have informally given them important information at different times and in different places; for example, in the form of small talk, with the expectation that the German will then put all of the pieces together like a puzzle. They themselves do not drop hints or share information informally; instead they bring their points together at the one time, at the appropriate venue, for example, a meeting, or in a memo or report. As a result, there are times when they are poorly or not at all informed about what is happening.

Direct Communication: No Double Meanings

During the first afternoon of an intercultural training session about Germany, the participants presented role-plays of their first impressions of Germany. They acted out scenes they considered to be typically German. One American woman together with the only male German participant presented the following scenario. She is living with her German boyfriend. After buying a new sweater in the city, she tries it on and asks him, "How do you like my new sweater?" He thinks it's really ugly and answers, "Uh, to be honest, I think it's ugly." Everyone laughs and says, "Exactly! That's just what happens. That's so typical." The German in the role play is puzzled and asks the American, "Why is this funny? What should I have said?" "Well you know, something a bit more complimentary. Something like: Oh, that's the new fashion, well, it's very colourful- or anything in that direction." The German doesn't give up, "But why?" "Because I thought that you loved me." To that the German responds immediately: "Oh, if you'd asked me whether I loved you or not, I would have said yes. But you asked whether I liked the sweater!"

It is the job of a Spanish project-leader working for a software system to test out various software programmes he receives. An engineering group has delivered a new product to test, which has serious weaknesses. During a meeting, the Spanish project leader vacillates back and forth about what he should say and in the end says that it could potentially be streamlined a little, and that perhaps some changes could be made. The German engineers understand his comments to mean just that: that the software, although potentially able to be further improved, is essentially suitable. The Spaniard becomes agitated: why don't the Germans understand that their work is clearly bad? As he tries to formulate what he wants to say, a German colleague comes to his rescue, and clearly and precisely states that this and that is simply bad and unacceptable. The Spanish project-leader winces and expects an emotional outburst, which, to his surprise, does not come. Instead the Germans begin discussing the weaknesses and their causes and the possibilities for improvement. An emotional escalation doesn't occur, and everyone discusses the situation matter-of-factly. The same words of criticism used in Spain would have led to deep feelings of anger, whereas the Germans have a matter-of-fact, albeit rigorous discussion, in which nobody takes the criticism personally. That afternoon everyone is smiling once again and drinking coffee together.

Being direct comes easily to Germans. They communicate on one level, with no room for ambiguity. A clear question gets a clear answer, without the frills and also without beating around the bush. Germans consider this to be the most honest, straightforward, authentic and believable way to behave. Being direct is especially important for professionals because it is goal-oriented, saves time, and cuts down on misunderstandings, and these are all very important values for Germans! This style is possible because the primary focus is clearly on the issue at hand (see *"Objectivism"*).

A Spanish manager has worked in Germany for two years in the research division of an international company in a very specialised area. The same position is currently open in Paris, and needs to be filled urgently. The German central office asks the Spanish manager whether he would be interested in the position in Paris, and they give him the contact information and hint how he can go about getting out of his current work contract. The Spaniard is completely astounded. The Germans he speaks with see only the position and are very matter-of-fact: they have to fill a position so they are looking for a person. If he can't do it, they'll look for someone else. They don't take into consideration any of the people – his boss or his colleagues – who could suffer from his transfer, nor that it could send signals to Spain that he prefers working in other countries, and so on. How can the Germans be so undiplomatic and inconsiderate of others?

If Germans do try to lessen the impact of criticism, they usually say something like, "Well, if you want my opinion, then . . ." or "To be quite honest, I think …. ." The criticism then follows honestly and clearly. When Germans fear that their opinion may upset someone, they will say that it should not be taken personally, or that it is important to look at the situation objectively. Requests and orders are softened through the use of conditional words such as "could" and "would," or the use of "please." This is how Germans show politeness and consideration whilst simultaneously meeting their high standards of honesty. Germans seldom say anything just to improve the atmosphere, except maybe at the start of a romance, nor do they pay false compliments or overdo politeness, as this smacks of hypocrisy and falsehood. People who are not completely honest and straightforward will be handled cautiously or even mistrusted: "What does he want? What is his real purpose?" A Korean, already living in Germany, whilst giving tips to his countrymen, summed it up as, "These people don't lie. They don't have two separate approaches for talking and thinking, so you always know what they are really thinking. I don't think the term 'hidden meaning or agenda' exists in Germany."

German helpfulness is usually only offered when asked for, so anyone needing help or information must clearly say so!

An American wants to buy a small screwdriver in order to repair her walkman. She goes to the watch and clock department of a large department store and asks the assistant where such a tool might be found in the store. The man simply answers, "Sorry. You can't buy that here. We don't sell screwdrivers." Without another word, he turns around and returns to his work. The American had actually expected that he would have given her a tip as to where she could find such a tool in the city. She is annoyed with the rude man, and wonders how the store can stay in business with such poor customer service.

Mrs. Smetana has only been working in Germany for a short while, and sometimes still needs help with her German from her German colleagues. One day she asks a German colleague to help her with the wording for a document. He answers, "I can't help you with this problem right now, because I don't have the time." She is upset and annoyed and thinks he is unfriendly and not very nice.

Germans are continually pressed for time (see *"Time-planning"*): it is a fact they openly admit to. The German answer, "I don't have the time," is almost never taken as it is meant by non-Germans (I don't have time *right now*), but is interpreted as a cold, hard rejection.

While shopping one Saturday, a Frenchman meets one of his nice German colleagues and his wife. They chat for a while on the street, until the German says, "Do you know what, I'm hungry. Shall we go to the pizzeria over there?" The Frenchman agrees. After everyone has finished eating, the German pays for himself and his wife, waits for a moment, and then asks the Frenchman if he's ready to pay. The Frenchman goes ahead and pays, but is upset. He had understood the suggestion to be an invitation.

If a German does not explicitly express such an invitation ("You are my guest" or "This goes on my bill"), then they are not, in fact, inviting you. On the other hand, if a proper invitation is made, they do not engage in polite argument about who should pay as, in their mind, this is clear.

A Chinese businesswoman visited friends in Bavaria, whom she has known for a long time. Although she knows that Germans seldomly invite acquaintances to stay the night, she was asked to stay and was invited to eat with them. Since she really enjoyed her visit, she had the idea of visiting her friends every year. Every time she happens to be in the area, she stops by and invites them to go out to a restaurant, which they always gratefully accept. The Chinese woman is, however, astonished that her German friends always let her invite them out and never think to invite her.

In the language department of a German educational institute, Chinese students are complaining that they are not receiving anything to eat from their German host families. The head of the language department is very puzzled and decides to look into the matter. She finds the following typical situation. A student comes home and the host mother asks her if she would like something to eat. The student politely declines. The host mother is disappointed that the Chinese student doesn't like the food and then offers her something else. The Chinese girl politely declines again. The host mother has something else in reserve and offers yet another option. The Chinese girl still politely declines. Every rejection is accompanied by words like, "Please don't make a fuss. I'm really not hungry." Well then, the host mother thinks, she really isn't hungry. And, once again, the Chinese student doesn't receive any dinner.

Similar scenarios can also be found, albeit to a lesser degree, between Germans and Eastern Europeans, whose attitude in such cases is that they should have been pressured a bit more before accepting.

A tip for non-Germans: do not try to interpret what lies beneath a German's statements. The message formulated is the message intended. This is also true for written messages and letters from Germans. They, too, should never be interpreted as meaning anything other than what they clearly say. The intended contents of the message are there, in black and white. Nothing more and nothing less.

Explicit Communication: Whatever Is Important Will Be Verbalised

Germans are often described as people who, in a professional setting, explain everything exactly and in great detail, without first checking to see whether or not their non-German partners really need or want all of this information.

There may be many different reasons for this:

– Perhaps the German merely wants to make sure by careful explanation that everything will run smoothly. They may feel that the foreign colleagues need to know everything about a situation – the background, causes and associations – in order to deal with it properly.
– Perhaps they want to show and demonstrate their competency, and make it clear that they have reached their position because of expertise and professionalism. Extensive explanations allow them to look good and demonstrate their knowledge of the subject.

A Swedish professor has German exchange students in her seminar again, just like every year. She has come to expect that when Germans raise their hand they will speak for several minutes long in order to pose a relatively simple question. In her view, the Germans are not really concerned with the question, but rather with the opportunity to put themselves in the limelight.

– All participants are expected to sit and listen to the information at hand even if only a few of them are directly involved. This is to ensure that everyone will be equally informed. (People with a different communication style may view this as an extreme waste of time.)
– Germans may offer a massive amount of know-how in a prepared written or oral format in order to show that they are open and prepared for cooperation.
– And last but not least, Germans always request that everything be put in writing: they like minutes, memos, documentation, notes, and so on.

The common denominator in all of these situations is that a situation is only considered "finished" once it has been explicitly discussed and brought to a conclusion. Since Germans prefer clear-cut communication, anything that you write will be highly valued: whatever is important is written down.

The way in which Germans build up and care for their relationships is also explicit. Speech expresses the reality. Germans say what they want, what they intend, which point of view they have and how they feel. In a nutshell: Germans define their situation for others through words and assume that the listeners will take it seriously and react accordingly. For this reason it is possible for individuals to get to know each other through conversation, in which they reveal aspects of themselves. If both people find themselves in agreement on enough themes, trust and friendship can develop. Relationships are established through speech and the exchange of opinion. Close relationships especially are based more on what is spoken than just the fact that the people are in close physical proximity. Germans do not feel that speaking about how they feel for each other will ruin a relationship: on the contrary, they feel compelled to do this, as they believe that speaking openly and with emotion will make a relationship closer and more trusting. Germans are happy when they can talk to someone, usually a close friend, about everything, even uncomfortable, problematic topics or their own mistakes and weaknesses. People from more implicit cultures (that is, with a more indirect style of communication) often think the German style of communication destroys everything that is dynamic and exciting in a good relationship: according to Russians, so much verbalising kills the feeling. For Czechs it is more like "someone being dissected alive."

Amongst Germans, the more people trust each other, the closer they become *(see "Regulation of Distance")*, and the sooner they will express their opinions and share their feelings openly and honestly.

Because of their explicit communication style, it is very difficult, if not impossible for Germans to recognise the "context" signals that people from other cultures use. When decoding a conversation, they only recognise and analyse what was expressly said. Hints, allusions and side references will be missed. It is alien to a German that such signs could actually carry the main message and be a normal way of communicating. The assertion "But I told you that," is accepted as true only if it was actually formulated that way when first said, during a conversation on the appropriate theme. Casual remarks or any other kind of informal information (see *"Separation of Personality and Living Spheres"*) will probably not be understood or registered. Germans do not take particular notice of the conditions under which a statement was made, nor do they interpret behavioural cues as an integral part of the message. According to German logic, only that which is spoken is relevant to the content of a conversation.

German managers in the Czech Republic are always complaining that their Czech workers resign without ever expressing any complaints or dissatisfaction. When the Czechs are asked why they didn't voice their problems earlier, they say the same thing over and over again: but we've been showing our dissatisfaction for months! Can't they see that our spirits have been low, we don't talk informally anymore, we don't make our offices look friendly and personal and so on.

A group of Hungarian co-workers are in Germany in order to learn about a new software-programme. Their German colleagues plan a group sightseeing trip to a romantic neighbouring city where they can take a boat tour and then go to a beer garden. They also organise the financial side, so that they can formally invite the Hungarians. The weather is supposed to be beautiful, so the Germans suggest taking the trip today. The Hungarians agree, but at 6 p. m., only the Germans are ready and waiting at the meeting point. They wait, but the Hungarians don't come. The whole next morning the Hungarians say nothing about why they didn't show up. By lunch-time the Germans can't take it anymore and have to ask, "Where were you yesterday? Why didn't you come?" The Hungarians say they went back to the hotel and went to bed early. Learning to use the new software and constantly having to do everything in German has been very exhausting for them this week. The Germans are flabbergasted! Hadn't they made an arrangement for yesterday? Oh well, that wasn't quite so clear to the Hungarians. What should they have said, other than yes, to such a friendly gesture? Other than that they hadn't shown much enthusiasm, which meant that the Germans should have realised that they weren't really interested. After all, no-one spoke further about the idea all afternoon, and one of the Germans had even given one of the Hungarians a headache tablet, which should have been a signal of how worn out he was, as were the others as well.

An Australian couple have become really good friends with their German neighbour. The German neighbour soon learns that he is welcome to drop in on the Australians at any time without notice. He really enjoys doing this. He often pops by in the evenings. To the chagrin of the Australians, he never notices the signals they give him suggesting when it's time for him to leave. Even if someone becomes restless, or gets up and starts to work, it isn't seen by him as a signal for him to go home. One day the Australian man loses his patience and says in a way that for him is bordering on rude, "It's really great to have you as a friend and to spend so much time with you, but right now we have something we must do. Would it be too much to ask you to leave?" This isn't a problem for the German at all! He thanks them for the clear message, says goodbye until next time, and goes home.

Whilst it is true to say that Germans read too little into the messages of others, they also fail to think about the implicit messages they could be sending. If you ask Germans for their opinion, they give it. They do not consider the impact their statement might have in a *particular* situation nor do they consider that their position of authority could also play an important role in how the message is received. Germans assume that anyone who disagrees will say so, as it is acceptable or even desirable to express differences of opinion. Germans are often astounded by the impact of their words.

A German managing a group of Czech employees is in charge of his company's stand at a trade fair. The stand is located in the large hall directly next to the entrance, an extremely favourable position. Unfortunately, the entrance consists completely of glass, the weather outside is unusually warm and the air conditioning isn't working. Everyone is sweating and at some point quite late in the afternoon the boss says, "It's unbearable in here!" The next day the boss can't be at the stand until the afternoon and when he gets there, it's gone! He finally finds the stand at the back end of the hall. Utterly furious he asks his Czech workers what they have done. The answer he gets is that they arrived very early that day and moved the stand to a shadier spot. During the heated discussion that follows, the German asks, "Who on earth decided that we should move the stand away from the great position we had?" "You did!" came the answer.

Conflict Confrontation

Especially surprising and, to some, possibly even frightening, is the way Germans communicate in the context of conflicts, discussion of problems and the sharing of unpleasant news. Germans are often seen as being very confrontational and completely unafraid of conflict. They point out mistakes, express criticism, identify and analyse problems and difficulties and come forward with their opinions in arguments. In short, they confront both themselves and others with conflict, and do not see this as a bad thing, but as a way of highlighting and addressing problems. Germans demonstrate their openness for conflict in the following manner.

Assertiveness

Germans are assertive and will defend their position. They value the sharing of opinions, and are prepared to disagree and reject ideas in a straight-forward, clearly worded way which may be seen as impolite. When Germans want something they ask for it directly, which may be interpreted by others as being demanding. They like to debate and seek out errors in logic, vagueness and inconsistencies because they are convinced it will help uncover the truth. One of the most difficult lessons for Japanese people getting used to Germany and attempting to be accepted by their business partners is learning to state their opinions loudly and clearly and being prepared to defend a viewpoint. Unless they do this, they are not taken seriously by their colleagues, or the authorities with whom they come into contact.

Germans are very clear and use a simple "no" if they do not want something or cannot do something. Saying "no" is not considered impolite, but rather a statement that prevents misunderstandings.

Similarly, Germans voice it clearly when they have a different opinion. Of course, they sometimes object faster than they can possibly have listened! Germans are even prepared to state their complaints and dissatisfactions directly to their bosses.

Many people find discussions with Germans to be quite aggressive. If Germans do not support something, or can see problems or mistakes, then they say so. The matters at hand are fought out, each person taking his or her own position whilst their opponents defend their positions. Thus, controversial points are decided by strenuous argument, which can be particularly traumatic for Asian colleagues. Germans openly express their feelings and opinions with a clear voice and with body language which cannot be misinterpreted. It is acceptable to question others and provoke argument and objections. In a group discussion, in which a solution is being sought, it is considered unprofessional and cowardly *not* to voice a differing opinion.

Germans believe that their discussion style is task and goal oriented: it increases the likelihood of all relevant factors being taken into consideration in the process of arriving at the best possible solution. In this sense the following is basically true: everyone can, may and indeed should state their opinions. How much of an influence this opinion will then finally have is, of course, not clear. The answer depends upon the context, the persons involved and the strength of the argument.

An Englishman living in Germany is participating in a meeting in which a decision has to be made about the next step in a technical development. He is shocked by the Germans' tone of voice: the group leader has a very strong opinion, and he pushes it with absolute conviction, "It has to be done this way, because . . ." Another colleague, an obviously experienced engineer, disagrees energetically. They argue, in what is for the Englishman, a loud and aggressive manner.The other participants become increasingly quieter and eventually do not say anything at all. In the end the team agrees with the group leader's suggestion. The Englishman shakes his head and wonders how it is possible for the Germans to speak to one another like that.

In conflicts, it is important to be tough and be prepared to fight it out verbally. If an agreement is reached, the fight is instantly over, and the solution that everyone has come up with will then go into effect *(see "Rule-Oriented, Internalised Control")*.

Mary Smith, an Englishwoman, works in a translating office whose business it is to accept customers and then distribute the work to sub-contractors who then do the actual translation work. One day a customer gave her a certificate to translate. The next day he returns and informs her that he no longer needs the translation. Mary can't return the document to him, because the translator has already received it and is working on it at another location. After she explains this, the customer becomes annoyed and yells that he can't understand why the certificate is not there! He won't pay! In shock, Mary retreats behind her counter. Luckily, a German colleague comes to her rescue. Her message to the customer is the same, but more assertive. The customer continues to curse and complain for a while and the German colleague responds, also in a forceful tone. The customer finally agrees that no other arrangement is possible and agrees to pay.

The relationship between a British personnel manager and one of his colleagues has been strained for a while. The personnel manager feels under severe pressure from the German who provokes him every time they meet. The personnel manager decides that he isn't going to put up with this aggression any longer, and is prepared to take drastic measures. One day the German calls and complains yet again about various processes, and takes the chance to criticise the Englishman. It seems that the moment for a counter-attack has come. After a grave pause the Englishman says, "I haven't changed my mind. Now listen to me," and with that he spoke his mind. There is another meaningful pause, then the German says "I've finally got to know you. Now we can talk straight with each other." The Englishman can't believe his ears.

Dealing with Criticism

Germans do not shy away from criticism, but express it relatively openly and honestly. They say exactly what they do not like and why they do not like it. They view criticism as serving objective goals: through "constructive criticism" they are merely pointing out a mistake or poor workmanship, and do not intend offence to the person responsible. Consideration of social factors such as personal sensitivities, age, sex, or whether anyone is really interested in receiving this piece of feedback all appear to be relatively unimportant from this vantage point. Hence, a particularly friendly introduction to a critical discussion appears more hypocritical than useful.

There is a saying in Germany: *Silence is praise enough.* This means that there is an assumption that everyone has done their best (see "*Rule-Oriented, Internalised Control*"), so a job well done does not need to be remarked on, instead it is only the weak points which are singled out so improvements can be made to achieve perfection. If there is no feedback, it is safe to assume that everything is satisfactory: no feedback is positive feedback.

Naturally, even Germans appreciate positive recognition and this style is also being taught nowadays in management seminars. However, giving exaggerated praise for every little thing is just not part of German culture. If praise and reinforcement are sought, it may be necessary to "put yourself in the limelight."

Indian software engineers are developing a part for a product that is to be assembled and distributed in Germany. There is a deadline for finishing the product. However, an important part of the information that is going to be given to the customers, and that the Indians need for the development, is apparently delayed in Germany and will not arrive in India until a month later than planned. The Indians work extremely hard, taking no time off, in order to bring the project up to speed so that the original deadline can be met with as little delay as possible. But the matter is complicated and the end product is sent on its way to Germany two days after the deadline, finally arriving there after a two-week delay. The Indians receive an unfriendly reply from the Germans in which a few relatively unimportant weaknesses in the part are pointed out. There is no word of thanks, no word of appreciation, no word of understanding for the transport difficulties from India to Germany, just criticism. The Indian crew is disappointed and feel like they have not received proper acknowledgement for what they have accomplished.

Seeing something critically is often regarded as a sign of intelligence and expert knowledge. Anyone unable to field critical questions or be sceptical must be unaware of the true complexity of a matter. Since nothing is solely positive and pure enthusiasm is just plain naïve such people are widely seen in Germany as being shallow.

In a talk show a Swedish director and several German film critics are discussing the Swede's latest film. To the astonishment of the Swede, the Germans don't just ask him questions, they attack his feelings: why did he do this or that? Why did do it this way and not another way? What did he mean with this? Why hadn't he considered this or that? and so on. The Swede, who thought he would be able to talk about his film, feels increasingly more uncomfortable and becomes quieter and quieter. He feels the Germans are very aggressive.

Problem Solving

If a problem needs to be solved, Germans are convinced that this is best done through relentless problem analysis and merciless addressing of weaknesses. Problems need to be recognized before it is possible to find good solutions and subsequently optimise products and procedures.

The way Germans deal with problems amazes many people. In terms of the *"Rule-Oriented, Internalised Control,"* it is important on the one hand that people recognise their mistakes, but at the same time they should not give the impression of being unreliable or disorganised. This is why people justify their actions and explain clearly how they came to make a mistake. This helps to save face and eliminates the burden of being solely responsible. It also serves to detect who or what was originally at fault. Such problem analysis can also be a learning tool for preventing future errors, rather than a way of avoiding blame or putting it on someone else.

In a collaboration between Indian and German engineers, mistakes are continuously occurring, but it's the way the Germans react which is really upsetting the Indians. They spend a great deal of time and energy trying to find out where something went wrong, sometimes even calling an extra meeting in which the mistake and the history of how it occurred is gone through, blow by blow. Only after this is done will they go to work actually correcting the mistake. Why isn't the first priority actually fixing the mistake?

Germans think about the *best* way to deal with problems and mistakes:

1. First of all, everything possible should be done to avoid problems in the first place. If an appointment or a deadline cannot be kept, than Germans expect that the people in charge will clearly say so (see *"Rule-Oriented, Internalised Control"*). This may create conflict, but it is seen as constructive since it is for the good of the common goal.

2. When a mistake has already occurred, a thorough analysis must take place. Assuming that all task parameters and professional competencies were clearly defined, it is possible to check what went wrong and who was responsible. Only then is it time to analyse and discuss the problems themselves, from an objective point of view. This process of inquiry continues as long as it takes to get a satisfactory explanation. The fact that the people involved may find this process unpleasant is seen as a necessary means to the end. Only when they are prepared to be self-critical and acknowledge their mistakes is it possible to deal with problems in a fast, efficient and cost-effective way, as resources are not being wasted in "cover-ups" and detection. Whoever is capable of admitting a mistake is considered committed because they are more concerned with the objective task than with saving face.

3. The mistake must be fixed as well as possible,

4. and adjustments must be made to avoid the same thing happening again.

The chief reason for many German team meetings is to carry out such analyses and to find possible solutions for both large and small problems. Committed colleagues engage in such difficult discussions, even if they do not know each other well and have little to base their relationship on other than the problem at hand. This is a good way of showing professionalism.

When Germans Use a Higher Context

To people from almost all other cultures the direct communication style of Germans can seem very impolite, extremely demanding and (in the case of one's boss) authoritarian. Time and time again, they are seen as being anything from hurtful to arrogant, occasionally heartless and cold in their directness, and definitely as lacking in charm. Germans appear to be interested only in their current objective goals, and many people regard them as being limited in scope, because they do not understand hints and allusions. They are convinced that Germans *intentionally* do not want to understand them, which leads us back to the accusation that Germans are cold and hard. There are, however, benefits to this style once it is familiar; for example, the absence of double meanings: one always knows exactly where one stands.

Of course, even Germans do not say everything, and they too expect the obvious to be understood, especially where there is a common base of information. This manifests itself in the fact that relationships are built up, defined and interpreted without this process ever being acknowledged and spelled out (see *"Objectivism"*).

- Generally speaking, context is much lower in German communication than in that of many other countries, and relative to the high context style of Asians, is almost non-existent. The multitude of non-verbal, indirect signals and ways of implying something which are normal for Asians are *not* normal for Germans.
- The German use of context, in as much as it exists, is more concerned with the *indirect context* than the *implied context*. This can be seen in linguistic structures such as conditionals (would, could, etc.), question forms and politeness markers.
- One of the few examples of implicit communication or a high level of context in German behaviour is during the process of coming to an agreement. Germans often expect agreements to be explicitly reconfirmed. They wait for all of the separate details of the agreement to be restated, and if this does not happen, they may see it as a signal that agreement has not *really* been reached.
- A stronger context can also be seen when problems arise. In such situations, true opinions are not always expressed. Depending upon the relative positions in the hierarchy, how the boss is regarded, or the existence of any personal relationship, Germans will decide whether to speak honestly or bite their tongues. In other situa-

tions, honest expression of an opinion can affect office politics, as certain aspects may be interpreted as a criticism of someone.

- There are many different situations in which Germans avoid conflict: for example, some employees strive to conform, are exaggeratedly obedient and submissive, or take pains not to be noticed, especially in times of high unemployment and when people feel insecure about their workplace.
- Germans criticise others, but can be quite sensitive to being on the receiving end themselves, despite the separation into different life spheres and the objective manner in which criticism is given. They do not always manage this as well as they would like!
- Not every conflict is motivated by the task orientation and objectivism. Some conflicts resemble a permanent battlefield and are never resolved. In such cases, the topics that are officially being discussed or fought about only serve to hide the real source of conflict (for example, a personal emotional conflict or a struggle for power).
- Germans are quite aware of the difference between constructive and destructive criticism. Constructive criticism concentrates on the subject at hand and does not aim to wound, whereas destructive criticism is often aimed at a target.

The Pros and Cons of the Culture Standard "Low-Context: the German Style of Communication"

An advantage of the direct style of German communication is that everyone is involved, not only those who have been part of the process from the beginning. Because essential information is explicitly and fully shared, it is possible to join in a conversation or a project part-way through.

This communication style provides the means of overcoming gaps in information and helps to integrate people into a group or team, thus making it easier to reach the common goal. It also makes it possible for people to know "what's going on." Germans state their requirements clearly, voice their opinions and say what they do and don't like. In this sense they are quite predictable. With their tendency to confront conflicts, problems can be identified, analysed and

185

then worked through in a goal-oriented way, and a solution can be found which will reflect the viewpoints of all involved.

The disadvantage of this culture standard is that everything has to be discussed completely and explicitly, which is often awkward, excessively detailed and lengthy. The clear, direct and undiplomatic way Germans have of saying what they think can be very hurtful to those unprepared for it – even amongst Germans! The fact that this pattern of communication is common practice does not mean that Germans cannot be hurt or insulted by it, but they probably do have a higher tolerance level.

People used to low context communication are inexperienced and unskilled in perceiving implied signals and do not know how to interpret additional non-verbal messages.

It is not common practice to use humour, for example, as a form of everyday communication in the workplace, since humour is based on some form of context, and often what is actually meant is not said. Of course Germans enjoy humour, just like everyone else, but it is reserved for very specific times and areas in life *(see"Separation of Personality and Living Spheres")*.

The disadvantage of confrontations is the lack of consideration shown for the feelings of those involved. The whole process of analysing mistakes is embarrassing to the person responsible for them, and can bring with it the risk of being labelled a poor performer.

Germans are generally allowed less leeway in their business dealings than their business partners from other cultures who enjoy haggling and doing business deals. The monetary guidelines are usually very carefully calculated and allow little latitude.

Recommendations

Suggestions for non-Germans Working with Germans:
- Express your needs, wishes, opinions and matters of concern verbally! Germans are unaware of ways of communicating other than with *non-ambiguous* words. They won't understand you if you use other signals to convey what you mean. Whatever you say, try to say it as clearly and directly as possible.
- If you feel misunderstood, recall "word for word" what you said. Was there any non-verbal message in the previous conversation

that has gone unnoticed by your German colleague? They may have ignored it as not being relevant.

- Don't search for any additional meanings or hidden agendas behind what Germans say. They express exactly what they wish to say – no more and no less. Answer questions just as they have been posed and don't assume that the question has a second, hidden level.
- Don't be reserved or slow in coming forward, but instead be demanding (in your eyes at least)! Say exactly what you want and need, without excessive politeness or self-deprecation. It's a good idea to make a deadline when you need something, because then you have a good reason to follow-up on your request.
- Voice a clear "no" when you do not want something and explain exactly why you do not want it. This is the best way to be convincing, clear and professional. Any kind of allusions, hints, tips or things that you have mentioned or referred to in a roundabout way will probably not be understood. Saying "perhaps" to be polite can lead to many more problems than a clear "no." If you do say "yes" then remember that it will be understood as a clear and complete agreement. You are destined to have difficulties if you didn't really mean "yes." When working with Germans remember that any kind of an acceptance is binding and is seen to be an obligation!
- Contradicting is not seen as a form of fighting, but is viewed as a chance to discuss the problem.
- If you haven't understood something because of a language barrier, don't hesitate to ask what is meant. Because Germans are direct, this is absolutely acceptable.
- Make dates and schedule appointments to discuss your issues. Once in a discussion, come directly to the point and say what your problem is. People will be glad to take the time to discuss things and work them out with you, since this is considered professional and responsible.
- Avoid making excuses. This is viewed as unprofessional and, at worst, can make you look like a liar.

On dealing with conflicts:
- Use objective argumentation, logic, agreements, contracts and laws to back up your position. On the other hand, compromises

can often save many a situation and can help both parties to understand each other on a personal level again.

- For the individual this means: *have courage!* Trust yourself to say what you think. Try to explain your viewpoint and make your position known in a very calm but persistent manner. In this situation it is best to avoid any form of aggression. Just say what you think. You will be surprised at how well this works: people who believe in and follow through with their objectives are respected! As a respected person, you will not be ignored and side-lined; instead, your opinion will count.
- When Germans criticise something (on an objective level) and discuss problems with you, it is a sign of their appreciation and respect for you. It means that they are taking you seriously as a colleague. They want to create a good cooperative working environment and work together to reach your shared objectives. Try to look at any criticism and all discussions regarding problems in this light. You may be pleasantly surprised!
- Inform all parties as soon as possible about a bad situation in order to avoid a possible catastrophe. Try to overcome the embarrassment this may cause you. If you don't do this, then the conflict that follows will be much worse and the situation even more embarrassing.
- Here are a few of the criteria that will help you see the difference between what a "serious objective discussion" with a German might look like compared with a situation in which a German is just trying to put you down. Anyone with a serious objective in mind:
  a) does not constantly question all points, but concentrates on the points that he or she is responsible for or has expertise in.
  b) uses the language of conciliation or compromise when making suggestions and statements.
  c) is not just critical, but also offers support and positive suggestions.

Suggestions for Germans Working with non-Germans:
- When working with people from different cultures be prepared for the importance of contextual cues. It's a good idea to take the time to create together a new *common context.*
- The more conversations that take place while working together,

the more the common context will be strengthened on both the objective task level and the emotional relationship level. This will also convince the other person of your sincerity regarding the partnership, and convince them of your commitment to offering mutual support and assistance. In this way you will also find out in time about problems and barriers that may exist and changes that come about, and therefore be able to react appropriately before a conflict arises.

Here are some tips to help you uncover what your colleagues may really be saying:
- Listen to the other person very carefully and without wanting to rush. Only then will you have the chance to understand what they want to communicate.
- Asking them for their opinion will also help! If you have even the smallest doubt that what you are being told is not the real and full message, trust your feelings and ask again. A "yes" is often meant merely as a polite gesture to appease the other person, or it may be said in fear or as a way of getting out of a discussion. Germans tend to be very trusting people, and in this situation it can be a disadvantage for them.
- When a problem is hinted at, take it seriously! A supposedly small problem may actually be big.
- Only by being open to discussion and by taking the time to speak to people will you earn the trust necessary for you to be included in the informal channels of communication. Listening to others and asking questions is expected from people at all hierarchical levels.
- German "low context" communication has a very strong correlation to the *"Separation of Personality and Living Spheres."* For this reason you must collect all of the different pieces of information you have been given at different times (regardless of which living sphere it was) and then put them back together like a puzzle. Always try to concentrate and register whatever meets your eyes and ears, no matter where you are. Observe the German W-rules: who said what, how, when and to whom, under which circumstances, what is the past history, what happened subsequently?

Be continuously aware of the contextual level and act accordingly:

- If you are the boss and wish to state your opinion, don't forget that because of your status and power: your words always have an effect.
- As a person you will be permanently watched and judged, even when you think it doesn't matter because you're not on the job. What you do counts much more than what you say. The impression you make is more important than the fact that you are fulfilling the parameters of your role. People from other cultures react more distinctly than Germans to the atmosphere that surrounds an individual.
- Keep in mind that, unless it's called for in a presentation, the detailed and structured preparation that is natural to you will be seen as authoritarian and excessive by others. There's the danger that your preparation will be seen as a flexing of muscles and a play for power, rather than a good base for discussion or an offer to cooperate. This is especially true when the German holds the more senior position.

Dealing with Conflict:
- In many cultures, problems are considered akin to conflicts and can only be openly discussed by people who have a strong and positive relationship.
- Therefore, only bring problems and conflicts out into the open if it is really important. In many person-oriented cultures the normal way of dealing with problems is to sweep them under the carpet so that they do not damage relationships. Unnecessary airing of problems and conflicts can actually make a situation worse than it already is.
- It is helpful to keep these rules in mind when giving any feedback, especially negative: speak in the first person, explain how you are personally affected, and don't judge the actions of the other person.
- Be very cautious of criticism on the personal level and consider the feelings of the other person. Constructive conflict discussions should only be held if the relationship is good, the atmosphere is free of fear so that the other person feels able to respond, and appreciation of the person's positive attributes is also expressed. A socially acceptable dose of criticism (not everything all at once!) is the right medicine to ensure a feeling of general well-being.
- Make objective criticisms very carefully, taking time to comment on what is good, and what could be done differently in your opin-

ion and why. Try to stay on the objective level, and avoid making the other person look bad through accusations of fault and guilt. The optimal way to formulate criticism is along the lines of, "I've got a few suggestions. This and that could be improved and I'm sure you can handle it."

Historical Background

Since the "low context" style of communication is a special phenomenon compared with "high context" styles found in other cultures, especially Asian, it is interesting to look at the historical roots.

There are ancient roots to the central place truth and truthfulness, and consequently directness, have in Western cultures. The search for "the truth" as an ideal existed in Ancient Greece. The concept of "truth" encompasses the attributes of eternity and rationality. Such higher maxims were not only aspired to for their own sake, they were also the basis for ethical principles.This is one of the foundations of Western thinking.

– European logic is an either-or-logic (Hofstede 1993): if there are two contradictory statements at least one of them must be wrong. It is imperative to establish who is right and who is wrong. Whereas Asians always try to incorporate the other side (because for them the "truth" is only one aspect among many and cannot always be pinned down), Europeans want to eliminate the other side completely. This way of thinking has particularly deep and strong roots in Germany. In the wake of the Reformation, the influence of the universities grew strongly, "... with the result that the development of an educational system, accessible to broad sections of the population became possible. Especially in secondary schools, classical languages and literature were a central component of the syllabus. The study of Ancient Greek and Latin and also of the philosophy of this time were accompanied by a heavy emphasis on the acquisition and use of logical thinking, and this continues in modern German secondary schools. Logical argument and debate in the tradition of the classical philosophers has, through the centuries, become part of the flesh and blood of Germans" (Markowski 1995, p. 54).
– Furthermore, there is the Western understanding of the cognitive

process "subject and object as the recognising and the recognised oppose one another in dualistic fashion" (Weggel 1990, p. 189). Cognition aims to objectivise the fact and to place it in context. Cognition implies the incorporation into objective context and freedom from subjective attachments. People from Western cultures prefer abstract terms and dissected thoughts, form categories and build systems, and can even construct whole edifices of thought or science on the basis of the interpretation of theoretical concepts. On the other hand, associations that are not of a causal nature present problems to Western thinking (Reisach et al., 1997). All of these historical roots cause members of Western cultures to approach things deductively, meaning they start with the core and work outwards, trying to deduct, for example, solutions to a problem. This requires a direct style of communication, since anything else could create uncertainty and irritation, which would hinder putting the statements of the other person into a logical context. In Asia, the process is quite the opposite: The objective must be subjectivised, following one of the tenets of mystical unification. The style of communication therefore emphasises induction and synthesis. In the 18th and 19th centuries, Germany experienced the blossoming of analytical philosophy, which radiated outwards from the education system into many sectors of the population, and became the basis for analytical thought and particularly systematic problem investigation.

Christianity followed on from classical antiquity as the new system of eternal and unalterable truths which could be perceived on an intellectual level.

- Christianity, having evolved from Judaism, also picked up many Ancient Greek traditions of thinking (the New Testament was originally written in Greek). Christian religion became dogmatic and intolerant of other belief systems. The perception developed that there was only one true way, for which dedicated Christians were prepared to suffer persecution and even martyrdom. Truth became the guide for action.
- Furthermore the Christians, motivated by the Hellenistic search for truth and the biblical command to "conquer the earth," set out on the road of thinking for thinking's sake, resulting in the great tradition of rational thinking. Misfortune was blamed in-

creasingly on natural and secular forces, the body was made available for medical research and rational concepts of time, space and causality evolved. In Germany, this development eventually peaked in the philosophy of Kant and the "Faustian thirst for knowledge" which Germans are said to possess. This thirst for knowledge could avail itself of the new philosophical methods of analysis, developed in the 18th and 19th century, which were more systematic than ever. Space for "irrationality" diminished.

– In addition, Christian religion had no accord with the supernatural. It lost many traditions of majesty and mystery and the Christian God increasingly developed into the rational and balanced God of the philosophers. Protestantism promoted this development even further with the result that the Protestant church service lacks cultic components in worship and spiritual offerings. Protestantism emphasises instead the intellectual sphere and rational thought, and increasingly suppresses emotional and irrational elements. For the style of communication under discussion, this implies the following: the foremost premise will be rationality; the search for and finding of the "truth."

This explanation does not suffice to understand why Germany, compared with other Western cultures, developed these characteristics in such a distinct way.

Because of political circumstances (the many *small states*), family and community relationships were bound by territory, and were stable and clearly regulated. It was important that the communication style did not endanger the relationships between people, so it was necessary to avoid ambiguity and to separate the objective, task related sphere from the subjective, personal sphere. A direct style of communication was the best way of ensuring this (Molz 1994). The existence of many small states meant that there were various "contexts" in Germany, which furthered this direct and explicit style of communication. People from different backgrounds had no common reference points and had to step beyond the boundary of their own context by systematically making their messages explicit and textualised (Demorgon 1999a). Such interaction was common in German culture, "as inheritance laws within the territorial families drove the larger part of every generation out of the family home and often across the boundaries of the small states" (Molz 1994), and "not even in early Germany when the Holy Roman Emperor ruled Germany, . . . was there a glamorous capital and residential city. The emperor was always on the move – from one Palatinate to the other, where he reigned and administered justice for a while, before moving on to the next residence, to the next jurisdiction with his entire court" (Gorski 1996, p. 131). German history has always been one in which the tribes and their leaders and, more recently, movements and their spokespersons have had to discuss matters in order to reach agreement if they wanted to practise successful politics. In addition "explicit communication also enhanced the success of cross-border trade in the merchant society" (Molz 1994, p. 117).

Protestantism also contributed to the low-context style of communication in that Luther's church was a church of the word (not of sacrament and liturgy) – the read, spoken, preached and sung word. The Protestant culture is a culture of the ear, the scripture and the book. Life is interpreted through the word, and reflection involves concentrating on the word (Nipperdey, 1991). This is an essential characteristic of explicit expression.

- Furthermore, Luther "eliminated the Catholic system of mediation and compromise between nature and grace, man and God, belief and world, the system of the analogies and syntheses of the 'and' and the 'as-well-as'. He is a man of 'either-or'" (Nipperdey 1991, p. 42). Clarity and certainty are called for.
- In addition, Pietism was a very influential Protestant movement in Germany, and Pietists were occupied with the search for the truth and unconditional truthfulness from man. The Enlightenment further intensified this expectation.

In such an ideological system there was no alternative to the search for the truth. Further understanding of the German style of communication can be gleaned from some *additional*, purely communication-related factors.

- Most Germans were strongly moulded by village life and from 1648 onwards, large areas of Germany had descended into provincialism and poverty. Contrary to the court environment, the style of communication in the villages was generally direct (Requate 1993; Kindermann). Even crude abuse and cursing were part of the normal repertoire, if honor was at stake.
- A sort of "agrarian citizen" evolved from the extensive urbanisa-

tion. Thus, in relation to the city milieu, Hellpach (1954) re-confirmed the maxim: "One does not expect anything else from a vassal other than being willing to work when on duty and being a boor in private" (1954, p. 211). This style of communication left its mark on broad sections of underprivileged city dwellers.

- Strangely enough, this direct style of communication was enhanced by the release of Knigge's book in 1788, which "marked the threshold of 'middle class' manners and forms of communication" (Requate 1993, p. 394): The form of communication used in the courts (based on pretense and flattery) was countered by Knigge with manners that, in the sense of the Enlightenment, were oriented towards personal responsibility and 'middle-class' virtues such as value, truth and honesty (Requate 1993, p. 394). These virtues are still mentioned today when Germans are questioned about the reasons for their direct form of communication.

- The German trait of expressing and formulating everything explicitly also serves the *"Appreciation for Rules, Regulations and Structures"*: "Everything that is set down explicitly, precisely, unambiguously and, wherever possible, verifiably, enhances the feeling that everything is regulated and results in the desired sense of order" (Molz 1994, p. 117). The underlying conditions which explain the value that Germans vest in structures and rules can also be looked at from a communicative viewpoint.

- A new era of equating direct communication with honesty and truthfulness arose in the 1960s. The 1968 Movement, in its attempts to overcome the terrible German past and to create a new set of values, brought about a new wave of radical openness, discussion and conflict, which swept through the country. This wave was fed through various channels: from a broad movement to democratisation to the understanding of group-dynamics. Large sections of the population endeavored for once and for all to banish the mentality that had contributed to the Nazi regime and to replace it with a different, fearless, more open mentality (albeit also of a confrontational rather than a compliant nature). Every type of "insincerity" and "ambiguity" was denounced and every attempt was made to avoid it. Since this time an important goal of education has been to instill in students the following: Be critical! Be sceptical! Learn to question! Do not accept anything that cannot be convincingly explained to you!

Me, me, me . . .

■ Individualism

How Germans are perceived by other cultures	
independent and self-sufficient; they have the freedom to do what they want	*Brazilians, Indians*
from a very early age, they lead their own lives	*Koreans, Spanish, Turks*
they often live as singles	*Indians*
family is not so important, there is little contact with parents, grandparents, relatives; there is a large gap between the generations	*Brazilians, Chinese, Indians, Koreans, Spanish*
close contact to the family, even as adults	*British*
strong sense of community (groups, family, clubs)	*US Americans*
everyone should state their opinion, personal opinions are important	*Japanese*
strong willed: one says no, contradicts, gets one's way	*Chinese*
work by themselves, both at work and at home	*Indians*
make their holiday wishes known and are usually granted, company-wide holidays are rather seldom; somebody is always on vacation	*Japanese, Indians, Spanish*
have a lot of keys, since everyone locks their things away	*Japanese*

In contrast to non-Western cultures, individualism is an important culture standard in Germany. Although this is a typical Western characteristic, and is even stronger in other countries, it is nevertheless different and distinctive for people from some cultures. I will describe how it is experienced by these people when they have contact with Germans. You may recognise many aspects of this culture standard because it underpins and influences so many of the other culture standards which have already been described.

Definition of "Individualism"

Individualism expresses itself in many ways, but the focus is always on the person as an individual. This may be seen in the relative emotional distance or independence a person has from group and organisational identity. Personal independence and self-sufficiency are highly regarded. The primary identity is the *personal* identity of the individual, which distinguishes and characterises the individual from all other people. The "motto" of this culture standard could be: "I am myself, I have my own goals and plans, as well as my own history and experience, therefore I am different from all others. I am unique. I make my own decisions in life. I have my own goals and interests, and when I make mistakes I take responsibility for them. I do the things I want to do, and which I think are right. I am the central point of my own life. I have to be happy and satisfied with my own life. No-one else's judgement of it is as important."

The right or, better yet, the *obligation* of each individual person to take responsibility for his or her own life plays an important role here. This is taken to the extreme in that every person is expected to maintain at least a minimum degree of autonomy from a group in order to remain psychologically healthy.

Individualism, however, does not mean egoism! The interests of an individual are weighed against the interests of the people around them, for example, partners, children, friends and community. What distinguishes egoism from individualism is the point at which the behaviour of one person has the potential to harm others, be it an individual, a group or a whole community. In Germany this "damage point" is marked by laws, regulations, contracts and agreements, and following these is therefore synonymous with fairness and consideration for others. Everyone has their own interests and rights, but it is expected that they will respect the interests and rights of others. Of course, as with small children, this does not always happen, and instead personal goals and interests are sometimes pursued without such consideration. Despite this risk, individualism does mean the freedom to hold on to personal interests and not have to give them up. For this reason individualism and the life-long self-sufficiency it denotes is a goal of the social organisations responsible for education and upbringing: people should be able to care for themselves as early and for as long as possible. An important prerequisite for achieving balance between the individual and society as a whole is the view that all people are equal, and that everyone can, and indeed must, take responsibility for themselves and their own interests.

Forms of Expressing Individualism

Individualism is often apparent at first sight. Each person experiences themselves as an autonomous being who must maintain a certain separation from others to preserve his or her own interests. The wish to be a little bit different from other people is frequently expressed externally, through striking or unusual clothing, distinctive behaviour, strongly expressed opinions, being outspoken about feelings, interests and preferences, or having very definite tastes for this or that consumer item.

The other side of the coin, of course, is that these signs of individuality are seen by others who will find them attractive or not, as the case may be. Such notes of individuality serve as an invitation to those who find them positive to come closer and get to know the person better.

From a very early age, considerable emphasis is placed on learning to think critically and becoming independent. Children must learn to have and to voice their own opinions, to make their own decisions and to do things alone. Today's secondary school students can even choose their own subjects. Germans can also choose what they want to study at technical and trade schools and universities. Studying demands tremendous responsibility and self-discipline. Adults are expected to be able to earn their own livelihood. It is also considered completely normal to be self-sufficient, for example, able to maintain a home and garden and undertake small repairs without assistance. This is not seen as degrading, but instead shows independence and is normal for Germans.

A group of Indians are role-playing several different scenarios they have entitled "working independently": Whilst doing his own photocopying, a German project leader makes a pot of coffee and pours himself a cup. After work he goes to a self-service petrol station and fills his car up, and once at home he spends some time repairing his car before mowing the lawn. In India he couldn't and wouldn't be allowed to do all of these things for himself. If he did he would be infringing on the territory and injuring the status of the many people whose full-time jobs are these very activities. He would also be damaging his own status.

Family life centres around the nuclear family and, within this structure, each individual's private spheres are respected by the other members. Children become independent from the family home at an early age and are relatively young when they move out in order to lead their own lives and assume adult responsibilities. Young adults make their own decisions about their courses of study, jobs, where to live and whom and when to marry. Parents and children visit one another, but it may be limited to a more distant host-visitor relationship, without strong connections. In the following example, a gesture meant as a compliment was misunderstood as a subtle criticism that someone was being too "motherly."

A newly-married Indian couple have been living in Germany for three years and have become friends with a young German couple. The four of them do many things together. They take sight-seeing trips on weekends, get together for a meal once in a while and the German couple have helped the Indians deal with many of the problems involved in settling in a new country, helping them buy furnishings and a car, getting their driving licences, and filling out all of the official forms needed by the authorities. They really like each other and the Indians are very grateful for all of the everyday tips their German friends have given them. One day, when the four of them are sitting together discussing the details of a small car repair job, the Indian man enthusiastically tells his German friends:"You are our German parents!" He immediately notices that he has said something wrong, because at that moment the two Germans look a bit shocked and say, "Oh! We apologize, we didn't mean it to be that way!"From this time on, the Indians have the feeling that the Germans have become more reserved.

A Chinese manager is celebrating Christmas in Germany with a German colleague.He learns that the mother of his host only visits during the holidays. She comes for one day and then goes home again. In addition, the Chinese man gets the impression that the mother is treated like a guest the whole time. A familiarity and intimacy is missing, and her behaviour is also very reserved. He simply cannot understand how a mother can be treated like this.

In an achievement-oriented society, asking for help may be regarded as a weakness and helplessness. Adults are expected to make sure they are properly informed and to manage things themselves. Anyone needing help will only get it if they expressly ask for it. To act otherwise could imply that the person being helped is considered incapable of handling their own affairs. A non-German wanting to offer help should first check beforehand by asking, "Can I help you?" If help is welcome, it will be signalled by a direct answer, "Yes." On the other hand, if help is not wanted or needed, it will be signalled clearly by "No thanks, it's not necessary."

Even salespeople in stores are cautious about asking the customers if they need help because they are walking a tightrope between offering assistance and information on the one hand and implying the customer is stupid enough to need unnecessary advice on the other. The desire to be independent and take personal responsibility is strong at all ages. Therefore, many elderly people want to continue living in their own homes, even when their children live far away. The loss of personal independence, such as when a person gets too old to take care of themselves, often leads to a feeling of worthlessness. In Germany old people do not receive special respect because of their advanced age.

A Chinese manager working in Germany meets an old woman on the street with a small shopping trolley on her way to do the shopping. Surprised, he asks her why her children aren't helping her, since this would be the completely natural thing to do in China. The woman answers, quite surprised, "But I can do it alone. Why should I let someone help me? Anyway, my children live far away, and I wouldn't want to trouble them, especially for such a simple little thing."

People try to keep relationships as balanced as possible, avoiding inequality such as dependency. This attitude can be seen in the way that Germans only give presents on certain occasions, such as to distinctly show appreciation of a favour. Even when friends go out together they usually pay for themselves, unless they have been expressly invited, otherwise an uncertain feeling of obligation or taking advantage may arise. Germans do not like to let themselves become too dependent on others. They want to maintain control over their own affairs in order to be able to discuss and make their own decisions.

An Indian woman who accompanied her husband to Germany is not allowed to work there. Twice a week she takes care of the daughter of a neighbouring family. Naturally she does this free of charge and it's fun for her to play with the little one. The two of them like each other. Yet she is continually receiving gifts from the little girl's family. In her eyes this is completely unnecessary.

An Indian engineer notices that not only do Germans talk in great detail about their ailments as well as those of their friends, but they also are very knowledgeable about all the details of the different diseases. They know exactly which symptoms to expect, what kind of remedies exist, the risks involved, as well as how the different diseases and remedies interact with one another. They appear to know a great deal and to have researched a lot about everything to do with health and disease. The Indian finds this rather excessive: isn't that why there are doctors and shouldn't one be able to count on them to take care of our health? Why should anyone want to learn how to cure themselves?

Ideal German employees are self-sufficient people, able to take responsibility for themselves and their work. Owing to their *rule-oriented, internalised control,* they are able to decide whether or not they can fulfil a particular role, and if they can, they will follow through with consistency. Unambiguous job descriptions and clearly delineated areas of responsibility actually confer a great deal of independence: people know exactly where the boundaries of their responsibilities lie and, within these, have a great deal of freedom, which is highly valued. If someone is unclear about what is expected of them, they request a meeting to clarify the situation.

In Germany, asking questions is generally seen as a sign of interest. There is a motto for this: "Every intelligent human being has questions!" German managers do not always take an active interest in the welfare or happiness of their employees. It is not their job to see how well their employees do their jobs: instead, it is the responsibility of the employees to fulfil their roles as well as possible (individual responsibility) and to report any difficulties to their manager (the obligation to inform: see *"Rule-Oriented, Internalised Control"*). In accordance with the *separation of personality and living spheres,* managers are not interested in the private lives of their employees.

The difference between acquaintances (groups to which a person belongs) and non-acquaintances (groups to which a person does not belong) is not as clearly delineated as in Asia or Russia. In Germany, closeness within groups is not so intense, and on the other hand the distance to strangers is not as great.

– Membership within most social groups is in principle voluntary: people who do not feel comfortable may leave the group. The one exception to this rule is the family. Close family contact in adulthood depends upon how well the members get along with each another. If they genuinely like each other, the relationships between parents and children can be very close. However, when the relationships are unhappy, there can be even more distance between family members than between friends and acquaintances.

– There are many types of groups to which an individual can belong: There are groups which are very binding and intimate because of their very nature, such as the (nuclear) family or a close circle of friends. The boundaries of these groups tend to be very rigid, and depending upon the circumstances it can take a long time to be accepted into them. Then there are less binding groups which have as their central focal point sports, politics, art, religion or some other interest or hobby. Membership in these groups is achieved more quickly, has a shorter time-span, is less intense and brings with it less responsibility. The goal or purpose of these groups forms the basis of relationships between members, and for this reason it is very simple to join in and become a member. In Germany, these groups are the key to making contact with locals and finding friends. If you are a non-German reading this book, I strongly recommend that you join a group involved in something you find interesting and enjoyable. Germans themselves know that such groups are a good way of meeting new people when they move or want to widen their circle of friends. People met in the workplace belong firmly under the headings 'profession' and 'role' (see the chapter on " *Separation of Personality and Living Spheres*") and are unlikely to become friends. In addition, what you may have known in your homeland as a neighbourhood is rarely found in the residential areas, large apartment blocks and cities of Germany. The wait to make friends in a German neighbourhood may be a long one. Closer contacts – more than just saying hello – can only be expected where there are common interests, for example sharing a love of gardening or because the children play together.

- There is no great distinction between people perceived as acquaintances and those perceived as complete strangers. Such people make contact on a 'distant' and functional level if there is a need. For example, it is appropriate to make direct contact with the person in the company who is responsible for an area in question without using an intermediary. No third party introduction is needed to smooth the way: on the contrary, often going directly via the official paths of communication is the best way to make contact. This direct approach applies for other groups, such as sport or interest groups, where the question "May I join?" is all that is needed. In Germany, it is not necessary to be picked up or be escorted in public, as taxi drivers and help desks are reliable. It is not necessary to have friends and connections within the medical system as health care is available for everyone. Information and the social infrastructure is also freely accessible. For these reasons, it is not necessary to be protected by a special group when pursuing individual activities. In Germany, there is a moral and legal obligation, which is by and large followed, to treat all people equally. Jobs are usually filled on the basis of qualifications, rather than internal contacts or friendships.

A Russian engineer is working temporarily in a German company. He is very surprised to find out that very few of his colleagues are related to each other. Over a year, he has only met one married couple who work for the company. Most of his colleagues work for one company and their partners and other relatives for another. In his company in Russia, on the other hand, many of the workers are related to one another.

In Germany there is a more abstract and anonymous understanding of community. This can be seen in the following examples. Flower-beds adorn large and small towns, and only drunkards would think of destroying them or picking the flowers. Germans are very willing to help in matters that affect the general public, such as environmental protection. When there is an appeal for money to help the victims of a catastrophe somewhere in the world, German aid and relief organisations are nearly always able to collect considerable amounts of money. There is a law that prosecutes anyone who fails to offer first aid assistance (no matter who it is) in an accident. Even in situations where it is clear that no one knows each other, like in the elevator or when waiting at a laundromat for the washing to finish, it is quite normal for greetings to be exchanged. The medical system is organised in such a way that there are always doctors and specialists on duty, and all patients can be sure of receiving care, even if their normal family doctor is not available. German drivers are extremely courteous towards pedestrians and will generally stop for them at zebra crossings. It is also true that most Germans are happy to assist or do small favours when asked.

Personal space is seldom shared in Germany and is highly valued. Maintaining personal space means keeping a minimum physical distance from others, having a private area or room, or having time alone free from the demands of others. For Germans, this is an important aspect of their psychological well-being. Even the private sphere of children is respected, and they usually have their own room and the privacy of their letters is respected. At work, people have their own desks, lockable drawers or cupboards, and maybe a personal office which can to some extent be individually arranged and decorated.

The general manager of a Chinese company is visiting a large German company. The German manager gives him a tour around the company to show him how they work. Whilst they are in the workshop, the Chinese visitor notices that almost all of the workers have small radios on their desks, that some people have flowers on their tables and that there is even a goldfish bowl. Also, a worker is celebrating his departure from the company by offering everyone coffee and cake during the coffee break. He can't understand why the bosses of the company tolerate such diversions during paid working time!

Guests in Germany are not constantly taken care of by their hosts. Rather, Germans assume that their guests are happy to have some time alone to do whatever they need or want to do. For this reason, hosts try to co-ordinate their own plans and appointments (see "Time Planning") with those of their guest.

A Russian woman working for a German company is sent to another city in Germany to work. Since she made a few friends in the first city where she worked, once in a while she returns to visit them on the weekend, but she can't get rid of the idea that she is a bother to them. She is always warmly greeted, and her friends always say how happy they are to see her, but then they all begin to discuss in her presence what they're going to do on the weekend. They each have a plan, which sometimes involves and sometimes doesn't involve their Russian guest. Sometimes they have to do something which excludes her, and she is left alone. Of course, since she knows the city, she can go shopping or do something else. "Make yourself at home! Feel free!" seems to be their philosophy.

A young Indian, who spent some time in professional training in Germany, has made friends with a German family. This family has repeatedly invited him to come and visit them during his holidays. The Indian plans to come during the summer, but the preparations, including the visa application, take far longer than he anticipates, and in the end his arrival date falls during the main German holiday season. He phones the family only to hear that they are sorry, but they have booked their holiday. He is more than welcome to stay in their house though, and they will leave a key for him. He should feel at home, enjoy the city and catch up with his other friends and acquaintances. They will be back two weeks later and can spend his final two weeks with him. When the Indian arrives he is very surprised to find out that everything is really the way his friends said! The family have gone on holiday, despite having a visitor! He stays in their house for a few days, then, bitterly disappointed, he returns home. He doesn't want to have anything to do with this family ever again!

Germans also see things that belong to them as a part of their private sphere. They are not keen to loan possessions, nor do they share their snacks and meals.

A Japanese man is disappointed in his German colleagues. They often eat or drink something while they are working, but not once has anyone offered him anything! He is continually sharing his snacks with others. Even during the breakfast break when he is just eating an apple he asks his colleagues if they would like a piece. They usually answer something like, "No thanks, I brought my own breakfast." Of course, he knows that everyone brings their own breakfast, he is just trying to be friendly and polite!

On a weekend field trip that has been organised by his company, where the employees and their families are invited, an Indian man is very disappointed at lunch-time to see how all of the families sit separated from one another on the grass. Every family has brought their own sausage, bread, and drinks with them. No-one seems to want to share with the others. The Indian expected a large buffet table where everyone would share their food and drinks with each other, and that everyone would then eat together.

Many of peculiarities regarding the German style of communication can be explained by individualism. The groups to which an individual belongs only give a rudimentary idea of his or her character: it is more important to listen to what they themselves say. A person's interests, opinions, convictions, principles, perceptions and values are what makes them who they are. These are the most important features of an individual. Expressing interests and standing up for convictions are important criteria for distinguishing an individual from other people: for giving this person a feeling of self and social identity, and giving others an idea of who it is with whom they are communicating. Communication is largely used in Germany to project an image of self (as defined above) in order to create or strengthen personal contacts with like-minded people. It is rarely used to create harmony in groups which come together randomly. In the business world this means that people show commitment and initiative by talking and asking questions. Communication transmits the speaker's feelings (even negative ones such as impatience, boredom, frustration or anger) and is proof of involvement, of being engaged.

Ideas, opinions, arguments and counter-arguments serve the dual purpose of helping to find a practical solution, whilst providing individuals with the chance to prove how serious, competent and hardworking they are.

Naturally, this assertion of individual interests and traits involves conflict and requires compromise: in short a way of handling competing interests and ideas.

– Conflicts can be solved by looking at the objective facts and the competing subjective interests. The cause of the conflict must be found, the different sides must be heard, the information must be fully discussed and a solution found which meets the objective demands and is not biased towards either side.

– Looking at the emotional level, Germans believe in "clearing the air" through honest expression of their feelings. Just as an explosion can be avoided by letting off some steam, emotions dissipate as soon as they are let out, and in the best-case scenario, after a fight all is forgiven and forgotten.

– If possible, conflicts should be resolved independently by the people involved. The use of a mediator is a sign of not being able to solve one's own problems. A boss should only be brought in to mediate after colleagues have tried and failed to solve a dispute.

– Being able to deal with conflict is an important goal of German upbringing and education. A person should be able to understand and weigh up different points of view in order to solve conflicts and find solutions.

Hierarchical relationships are constructed in order to serve a purpose: every society or company must have some sort of organisation, and a hierarchical structure provides this.

The roles and tasks everyone within the group must perform in order to achieve the common goals are clearly defined. There are times, however, when the idea of equality comes to the fore: either because of the demands of the task (for example, when the engineer crawls under the production line to check what's happening) or because of a private relationship between people at different hierarchical levels, or because there is a desire to create a "normal" and casual atmosphere at a time when the hierarchy plays no role.

An Indian notices that the head of his department often goes to lunch with his secretary. They both go to the normal cafeteria (not the one reserved for management), sit at a table, eat lunch and converse with one another. This is very strange for the Indian: why would a German boss go to lunch with his secretary? In India the cafeterias are separated and a secretary would definitely not be allowed to go into the same cafeteria as her boss.

A Korean goes on a skiing trip organised by the sports club of his German company. As it turns out, after everyone is put into groups according to their skiing ability, the Korean is the only beginner. Every group is assigned an instructor and to the astonishment of the Korean he gets the head of the ski club, who of course is a fantastic skier! The Korean is thrilled, but he does wonder how it can be that the head of the ski club is willing to forfeit his whole weekend to teach him? After all, isn't he entitled to a great skiing weekend?

"Individualism" and the Other Cultural Standards

Individualism is a fundamental culture standard in Western culture. For this reason I would like to show how this culture standard is connected to other German culture standards and why these connections are important.

The most obvious connection is between individualism, the moral basis of the legal system and the direct style of communication. The main principles are as follows:
1. *Individualism* stresses the dignity and the integrity of each person.
2. The border where the interests of one ends and the interests of another begin must be carefully marked and monitored by laws,

rules, and contracts (structures) so that everyone receives their due rights. These parameters are basically what holds society together *("Appreciation for Rules and Regulations")*.

3. Everyone (even high-ranking persons) must categorically comply with the structures that are valid for each situation. They serve as the basis on which society as a whole is built *("Rule-Oriented, Internalised Control")*.

4. With regards to these rules, respectable Germans are governed by a "principle of guilt," which means that someone who violates the rules feels personally guilty and regards their mistake as a personal violation against the community or society *("Rule-Oriented, Internalised Control")*. Avoiding being caught is not considered as being a particularly desirable and clever behavior, and lying is not admired as being cunning and intelligent. (It is, however, true that many Germans do not always, or only partially, obey rules and/or feel guilty when they have not obeyed them. Yet the fact that such violations are exposed and are branded as being wrong proves that these behavioural guidelines are still very much valued.)

5. A relatively direct style of communication is important (a) for negotiating new rules in the situation where there are opposing parties and the existing structures do not (yet) lay down the rules for dealing with the situation. In order for each person to be effective it is necessary that they be able to form their own opinions, be able to discuss both opinions openly, and be able to develop strategies in which a new set of rules can be set up so that the interests of both parties can be taken into consideration. People must also (b) be capable of dealing with conflicts, and be able and to know how to claim their rights when the existing structures have been violated *("Low Context: the German Style of Communication")*.

6. Furthermore, it is easier to get to the point because in a culture that is individual-oriented it is unnecessary to create or to check-up on the group feeling. The fear that differences of opinion could ruin the good positive atmosphere (group feeling) plays a much smaller role. Rather, communication is of a purely pragmatic character with regards to reaching an agreement *("Objectivism")*.

Recommendations

Suggestions for non-Germans Working with Germans

- Do not be too modest or too polite. Stand up for your interests and make reference to your performance. This is especially important when you are in the position of representing your company in Germany. Being reserved is not interpreted as being polite, but rather may be interpreted as reflecting incompetence. This is because you were brought here to represent the interests of your company. State your opinions loudly and clearly and with as much self-assurance as you can muster. Be prepared to explain and justify your point of view. Make sure you are put on the agenda. Never wait for Germans to solve your problems. Only then will Germans regard you as an equal partner who is equally responsible for solving the problem. Keep up the dialogue, talk to them and present your ideas!
- Do not expect to be continually accompanied, supported or helped. Everyone has their own responsibilities, and they probably have very little time for you. Besides, when you are sent out on your own it is a sign that you are viewed as being competent and as someone who can handle challenges alone. No one will understand your feelings that you had a right to more help. If you do need help in order to get your work done, the German motto is: you have to ask for it.
- In general it is better take the initiative. Ask your colleagues and acquaintances for information, invite them over or suggest doing something together and routinely make appointments with your boss in order to discuss matters that concern your work. This is the best way to make sure you will not be overlooked and you will be seen as being an engaged and interested employee. You will be viewed as a key player, someone who is interesting and energetic. (If you always wait until you are spoken to, then you will more than likely wait in vain.)
- Take everything that is written down seriously – contracts, minutes, signatures. They are considered as binding while informal agreements are of lesser importance.
- Take part in free-time activities. Simply find out the place and time of the meetings and go there (you do not need anyone to introduce you, you can go alone, women don't need to worry

about going alone either) and tell them that you would like to participate. After you have participated a few times, the contacts will become more open and friendly.

- Take into consideration that your German colleagues will have less to do with the rest of their families than you do in your country. Such obligations are not normal, and no one would understand you should try to argue your case for them. Should you have some sort of time-consuming family responsibilities, then make sure you tell your German bosses what you have to do and explain to them the importance it has in your culture.
- Take into consideration that it is more common for people to have relationships with people who are on the same level (horizontal) than with people on different levels (vertical). This means relationships with partners, friends, and colleagues are more personal and warmer than those with higher or lower hierarchical levels, which tend to remain more distanced and objective. Search for peers and do not be disappointed if your (professional) status is now and then disregarded. It is simply not regarded as being so important – at work one's hierarchical position is often of secondary importance *("Objectivism")*. In one's private life, however, one deliberately takes pains to keep the relationships on a horizontal level .

Suggestions for Germans Working with non-Germans
- Realise that for many of your foreign colleagues the time in Germany may be the first time that they have been really *completely* alone (alone in a room, for a whole weekend or for many evenings). This will help to give you an idea how much social contact is sought after and perhaps even missed.
- Try to understand and to adapt to your foreign colleagues as much as possible and, whenever possible, help them out and make them feel welcome. Talk to them at work, offer to help them with everyday problems, invite them to your home (it does not have to be anything special). Just *being* together is what is important!
- Take into account that personal relationships in non-individualistic cultures are the keys to personal and professional success. It really pays off to take the time to make personal contacts. Should you be successful in making such a contact, be prepared to assume a long-term position as contact person and spokesperson for

them and your company. If they come to trust you, they will want to talk to you about many things (not just those aspects for which you are responsible); equally, you can tell them about important matters in the company.

- Make the effort to give your visiting non-German partners the respect appropriate to their status. Attempt to have all business dealings with your guest be done by members of the same or a similar hierarchical level, and not via stand-ins or subordinates.

Historical Background

Individualism, a wide-spread phenomenon in Western cultures, has its cultural and historical background in the Judeo-Christian religion. It is here that the individual as an entity takes on great importance. The following points are deemed to have made the most significant contributions.

- Individualism is the flipside of Jewish monotheism, which demands exclusiveness (one cannot choose which God to pray to, because there is only one God). The plans this exclusive God has for the individual's life cannot be foreseen, nor can the Creator's behaviour be controlled by human rituals. Therefore, to be able to live life in a way that is pleasing in the sight of God, a relationship between the concrete individual and God needs to be established. This is the only way for humankind to know the will of God (Cahill 2000).
- Furthermore, the idea of the individual's responsibility towards his only God, widely laid down in religious law, weakens or limits the individual's ties to his family, local or ethnic group (Nipperdey 1991).
- Christianity goes even one step further: The historical figure Jesus, the man, is seen as God incarnate. This raises the status of mankind from "God's creatures" to "God's partners." Every human being, child or adult, rich or poor, suddenly becomes important and is considered "an image of God" (Mensching 1966). From then, the example of Jesus serves as the role model for all believers and gives everyone their unique, personal relationship with God, challenging them to live their lives like Jesus lived His (the main religious doctrine of the original early Christian believ-

ers). Love of God and love for one's fellow human beings (brotherly love) are inseparable. It is impossible to sincerely love God without loving one's neighbour as oneself and vice versa. This is a biblical law and one of nature's laws, deeply inscribed in all mankind.

Christianity was and always has been based on the conscience of the individual, despite the manifold ecclesiastical developments throughout the centuries. The commandments of The Love of God and Brotherly Love "love thy neighbor as thy self," are the binding religious principles on which everyone, according to the Christian faith, will be judged at death. Protestantism gave this ideology a new impetus. It was during the time that the Catholic church became an "institute of salvation" that supported and favoured a very static, organised, indirect and devout form of worship, that Martin Luther in his counter-movement began preaching the true original Christian attitude: The only thing that is truly important is to live with God or to live in such a way that it is pleasing to God and not some ritualised piousness. The resulting conscientious introspection lastingly promoted individualism in the sense of making one personally responsible for one's way of living and completing the individualistic development religiously. These beliefs are based completely on individual, personal and conscientious enlightenment and conscientious decisions (Kindermann). The effect of the Christian commandment "to love one's neighbour as oneself" put an end once and for all to the general particularistic disposition of preferring groups over individuals, since the "neighbour" refers to every person on the planet.

Around the same time as Luther, the philosophical and intellectual movements of Humanism (14th and 15th century), Renaissance (16th century) and later the Enlightenment (18th century) reinforced the position of the individual and resulted in the role of the individual – becoming even further refined and internalised. The definition of Individualism originated in the conviction that a human being as an individual is, translated from Latin, "inseparable," of a kind, a non-comparable entity.

Humanism – in its philosophical orientation to the world of the Greeks and Romans before Christ – stresses the value and the dignity of the individual, which is even evident in all aspects of the arts. During the Renaissance the ancient concept of individualism was rediscovered, and the attempt was made to contemporise this knowledge in the form of art, philosophy and law (Troeltsch 1925). The Enlightenment, postulating reason as its central aspect, brought about far-reaching philosophical, social and political changes in Europe. Thereafter it was expected that every person be educated and made competent enough to take responsibility for themselves and to lead their life in a self-determined, rational way. Reason in this context is to be understood as the God-given ability to think logically. However, as far as social life is concerned, should the individual concede reason to the politically powerful? The philosophy of Enlightenment demanded tolerance and equality be granted to all mankind in the eyes of the law, and at the same time it would be expected that all people would obey the law. Because of this change, the irreversible fate each individual had up until that point, dependent as it was on one's social class and religion, suddenly disappeared and social mobility became a reality. From a psychological point of view, the disintegration of the bonds that had up until this point been so strong, suddenly made the creation of one's personal identity an important issue: Who am I? What do I want? How do I get my share of appreciation? (Böhm 1995)

The Enlightenment had a lasting effect and was the factor responsible for altering all aspects of life thereafter, such as form of government, educational system, etc., and it imparted to the individual the responsibility and the rights to deliberately and conscientiously create oneself and one's existence. This applied, however, more to France and England than it did to Germany. Because of the political situation in Germany at that time (feudalistic, absolutistic mini-states), the Enlightenment had less of an effect in Germany than in other countries. This is the main reason why the characteristic trait of individualism is much more distinctly seen in other Western cultures than it is in the German culture. Because these various movements – Protestantism, Humanism, the Renaissance and the Enlightenment – had little effect in the orthodox regions of the Christian world, individualism has not been very pronounced in these cultures – despite Christianity.

The nuclear family, the single life-style, financial independence, etc., are all visible signs of individualism as a way of life. To a large extent, this kind of individualism is a completely secular phenomenon that has been driven to new heights by the capitalistic economy of the 20th century. Yet without the historical background mentioned earlier, this development would never have been conceivable or so fruitful. For this reason Hofstede sees a correlation between individualism and affluence: The more prosperous a country becomes, the more possibilities exist for the inhabitants "to do there own thing" (Hofstede 2000, p. 94).

I have called individualism a "fundamental culture standard." From the cultural perspective this also holds true: individualism has been a constant factor throughout both ancient history and Christianity, particularly during the Protestant movement. Consequently, statements concerning these two "foundation layers" may be found throughout this book and therefore they do not need to be rediscussed here.

■ Conclusion

"What now? What do I do now?" – These are the questions you may be asking yourself as we approach the end of this book. Maybe I have tried to share a bit too much information with you. Maybe our German culture standards seem to be written in stone, like hurdles which are impossible to overcome, unalterable for all eternity (or at least in your or my life-span!). Yet it was not my intention to confront you with so many details about the peculiarities of German culture and potential problems you may have working with Germans that you are incapable of acting. On the contrary: by giving you such detailed information about Germans, I wanted to supply you with a set of tools with which to understand and better communicate with Germans. The evaluation of intercultural training sessions has proved that it is our *knowledge* of a foreign culture that creates a solid foundation for intercultural learning and intercultural competence when dealing with foreigners: our emotions, perceptions, behaviour and the outcome are all influenced by this very *knowledge* (Kinast 1998).

The processes resulting from this knowledge are as follows:

1. First, you are able to *perceive* a foreigner's culturally divergent behaviour (that is, the behaviour that runs contrary to your expectations) as a result of his or her different cultural background, rather than falsely labelling it a personal quirk, or strangeness, impoliteness, incompetence or authoritarianism. This insight is the basis for the next step in understanding your counterpart.

2. The insight you have gained helps you to become and stay less *emotionally involved*, as you won't be feeling as overwhelmed and irritated by cultural differences as before. You will generally be less surprised, disappointed and antagonized by "foreign" behaviour. In certain situations, you will even be able to anticipate the other person's behaviour, so there will be fewer surprises.

3. This in turn results in your being able to *react* in a more relaxed,

controlled and appropriate manner. You are now in the position of being able to explain the reasons behind the foreigner's behaviour in specific situations. You may even succeed in responding to the foreign culture in a way that takes it into account and helps reduce the gaps between your cultures. You are now better prepared for an intercultural encounter; you are better informed, you are better "armed" and have more strategies up your sleeve. This reduces the danger of an intercultural encounter escalating significantly, because both sides will not resort to and stubbornly insist on their own cultural behaviour patterns being the "right ones"; nor will they make matters worse by retaliating for something that they have misinterpreted as a slap in the face. On the contrary: since cooperation is necessary to reach your goals, taking a step towards understanding the other person's position is the first step you need to take.

4. Knowledge about foreign cultures helps us to see the other's behaviour in a more positive light, and to *acknowledge* that it *is* indeed reasonable and sensible behaviour, albeit a bit exotic. This is not only more pleasant for the other person, it also makes it easier for you to continue the intercultural learning process. A positive attitude toward foreign cultures generally results in more open-mindedness and curiosity, and makes establishing social relationships with foreigners easier.

If you are a non-German reader, I hope I have supplied you with enough information about Germans to help you to understand them better. The related information presented is meant to give you suggestions for meeting your German counterparts halfway, leading to more successful interactions. You should now have the fundamental information necessary for taking the steps along this learning process to intercultural competence.

For my German readers I have discussed in a very condensed form many points which are already known to you. This book offers you hints about situations in which typical German behaviour may be seen as particularly extreme and where it might be better to restrain yourself and moderate your behaviour. After receiving this feedback, you may reflect how many severe intercultural misunderstandings can arise in situations where you have no idea that you are "treading on thin ice." You will have acquired a broad foundation for the first level of intercultural competence: the awareness of cultural divergence. To anyone who wishes to continue this intercultural learning process, I recommend that you collect more information about the culture you are dealing with.

My book will have fulfilled its intended purpose if both readerships have learned one thing: there is no other way to successful international cooperation than to accept diversity and work with it. Of course, there is no "one and only" strategy for handling all international cooperation: the appropriate strategy depends mainly upon the triangle of *situation* (the task at hand or the context of the intercultural interaction), the *people* involved and their *culture*. Real people want concrete solutions to a concrete situation – we are not talking about an abstract model of how abstract people succeed in solving abstract problems. Thus, intercultural exchange is not only indispensable, it should be embraced whole heartedly. If such an exchange is to be fruitful for both sides, it must be based on mutual respect, even – and especially – when the other person does not live up to our own expectations and values.

I wanted to supply you with the tools for understanding why Germans behave the way they do, but also to give you an insight into how this is seen by an outsider to the culture, whose definition of what is normal and expected behavior is different. The easiest response to intercultural misunderstandings is avoidance; the most dangerous is to dominate the intercultural situation via, for example, economic power; and the most challenging is to understand the differences and their causes. This last option is slow, strenuous and difficult, to be sure, but it is the only one that guarantees continuous, mutually satisfying relations between citizens of different nations.

■ References

Althaus, H.-J.; Mog, P. (1992a): Aspekte deutscher Raumerfahrung. In: Mog, P. (Hg.), Die Deutschen in ihrer Welt. Tübinger Modell einer integrativen Landeskunde. Berlin, S. 43–64.

Althaus, H.-J.; Mog, P. (1992b): Aspekte deutscher Zeiterfahrung. In: Mog, P. (Hg.), Die Deutschen in ihrer Welt. Tübinger Modell einer integrativen Landeskunde. Berlin, S. 65–87.

Althaus, H.-J.; Mog, P. (1992c). Zum Verhältnis von Privat und Öffentlich. In: Mog, P. (Hg.), Die Deutschen in ihrer Welt. Tübinger Modell einer integrativen Landeskunde. Berlin, S. 88–110.

Bausinger, H. (2000): Typisch deutsch. Wie deutsch sind die Deutschen? München, 2. Aufl.

Boesch, E. (1980): Kultur und Handlung. Bern.

Böhm, M. (1995): Analyse zentraler deutscher Kulturstandards in ihrer Handlungswirksamkeit in der Begegnung zwischen chinesischen Studenten/Sprachdozenten und Deutschen. Universität Regensburg: Unveröff. Diplomarbeit.

Cahill, T. (2000): Abrahams Welt. Wie das jüdische Volk die westliche Zivilisation erfand. Köln.

Craig, G. (1985): Über die Deutschen. München, 5. Aufl.

Demorgon, J. (1999): Interkulturelle Erkundungen. Möglichkeiten und Grenzen einer internationalen Pädagogik. Frankfurt a. M.

Dinzelbacher, P. (Hg.)(1993): Europäische Mentalitätsgeschichte. Stuttgart.

Elias, N. (1992): Studien über die Deutschen. Machtkämpfe und Habitusentwicklung im 19. und 20. Jahrhundert. Frankfurt a. M.

Engelmann, B. (1977): Wir Untertanen. Ein Deutsches Anti-Geschichtsbuch. München.

Gehlen, A. (1975): Einblicke. Frankfurt a. M.

Gorski, M. (1996): Gebrauchsanweisung für Deutschland. München.

Gross, J. (1971): Die Deutschen. München.

Hellpach, W. (1954): Der deutsche Charakter. Bonn.

Hofstede, G. (1993): Interkulturelle Zusammenarbeit: Kulturen – Organisationen – Management. Wiesbaden.

Kalberg, S. (1988): Aspekte des deutschen Verhältnisses von Privatheit und

Öffentlichkeit. Ein integrativer Versuch in kontrastiver Perspektive. Harvard University, Center for European Studies, Cambridge, MA: unveröff. Manuskript.

Kielinger, T. (1996): Die Kreuzung und der Kreisverkehr. Deutsche und Briten im Zentrum der europäischen Geschichte. Bonn.

Kinast, E.-U. (1998): Evaluation interkultureller Trainings. Lengerich.

Kindermann, H. (Begr.). Handbuch der Kulturgeschichte, Abt.1, Zeitalter deutscher Kultur. Potsdam.

Klages, H. (1987): Wandlungsschicksale der Identität der Deutschen: Ein Szenario der Wertwandlungen seit 1871. In: Weidenfeld, W. (Hg.), Geschichtsbewußtsein der Deutschen. Materialien zur Spurensuche einer Nation (S. 203–223). Köln, S. 203–223.

Krockow, C. v. (1989): Heimat. Erfahrungen mit einem deutschen Thema. Stuttgart.

Kroeber, A.; Kluckhohn, C. (1952): Culture: a critical review of concepts and definitions. Cambridge, MA.

Le Goff, J. (1987): Eine mehrdeutige Geschichte. In: Raulff, U. (Hg.), Mentalitäten-Geschichte. Zur historischen Rekonstruktion geistiger Prozesse. Berlin, S. 18–32.

Markowsky, R.; Thomas, A. (1995): Studienhalber in Deutschland. Interkulturelles Orientierungstraining für amerikanische Studenten, Schüler und Praktikanten. Heidelberg.

Mensching. G. (1966): Soziologie der großen Religionen. Bonn.

Molz, M. (1994): Analyse kultureller Orientierungen im deutsch-französischen Dialog. Regensburg: Unveröff. Diplomarbeit.

Münch, R. (1984): Ordnung, Fleiß und Sparsamkeit. Texte und Dokumente zur Entstehung der »bürgerlichen Tugenden«. München.

Münch, R. (1993): Kultur der Moderne, Bd. 2: Ihre Entwicklung in Frankreich und Deutschland. Frankfurt a. M.

Nipperdey, T. (1991): Nachdenken über die deutsche Geschichte. München, 2. Aufl.

Noelle-Neumann, E. (1987): Do the Germans have a ›national character‹? Encounter 3: 68–72.

Nuss, B. (1992): Das Faust-Syndrom. Ein Versuch über die Mentalität der Deutschen. Bonn.

Pross, H. (1982): Was ist heute deutsch? Reinbek.

Raulff, U. (Hg.)(1987): Mentalitäten-Geschichte. Zur historischen Rekonstruktion geistiger Prozesse. Berlin.

Reisach, U.; Tauber, T.; Yuan, X. (1997): China – Wirtschaftspartner zwischen Wunsch und Wirklichkeit: ein Seminar für Praktiker. Wien.

Requate, J. (1993). Kommunikation: Neuzeit. In P. Dinzelbacher (Hg.), Europäische Mentalitätsgeschichte (S. 362–399). Stuttgart: Kröner.

Sana, H. (1986): Verstehen Sie Deutschland? Impressionen eines spanischen Intellektuellen. Frankfurt a. M.

Sana, H. (1994). Unzufrieden und freudlos: Fetisch Perfektionismus. In A. Nünning & V. Nünning (Hg.), Der Deutsche an sich. Einem Phantom auf der Spur (S. 175–196). München: dtv.

Sauzay, B. (1986): Die rätselhaften Deutschen. Die Bundesrepublik von außen gesehen. Stuttgart.

Schroll-Machl, S. (2001): Businesskontakte zwischen Deutschen und Tschechen. Kulturunterschiede in der Wirtschaftszusammenarbeit. Sternenfels.

Thomas, A. (1988): Untersuchungen zur Entwicklung eines interkulturellen Handlungstrainings in der Managerausbildung. Psychologische Beiträge 30: 147–165.

Thomas, A. (Hg.) (1996). Psychologie interkulturellen Handelns. Göttingen.

Thomas, A. (1999): Kultur als Orientierungssystem und Kulturstandards als Bauteile. IMIS-Beiträge H. 10: 91–130.

Thomas, A.; Schenk, E. (1996): Abschlußbericht zum Forschungsprojekt »Handlungswirksamkeit zentraler Kulturstandards in der Interaktion zwischen Deutschen und Chinesen« Regensburg: unveröffentl. Manuskript.

Troeltsch, E. (1925): Aufsätze zur Geistesgeschichte und Religionssoziologie. Tübingen.

Wagner, W. (1996): Kulturschock Deutschland. Hamburg.

Weggel, O. (1990): Die Asiaten. München, 2. Aufl.

Wenn Sie weiterlesen möchten ...

Sylvia Schroll-Machl
Die Deutschen – Wir Deutsche
Fremdwahrnehmung und Selbstsicht im Berufsleben

Die Globalisierung ist inzwischen allgegenwärtig. Diese
Tatsache stellt viele Menschen vor neue Situationen: Kulturunterschiede sind nicht mehr nur etwas, was Touristen
fasziniert und Wissenschaftler anregt, sondern sie sind weit-
gehend Alltag geworden, insbesondere auch in beruflichen
Zusammenhängen.

Das Buch wendet sich an beide Seiten dieser geschäftlichen
Partnerschaft: zum einen an jene, die mit Deutschen von
ihrem Heimatland aus zu tun haben, oder als Expatriate, der
für einige Zeit in Deutschland lebt, zum anderen an die Deutschen, die mit Partnern aus aller Welt im Geschäftskontakt
stehen, sei es per Geschäftsbesuch oder via Kommunikations-
medien. Für die erste Gruppe ist es wichtig, Informationen
über Deutsche zu erhalten, um sich auf uns einstellen zu
können. Für Deutsche selbst ist es hilfreich zu erfahren, wie
unsere nicht-deutschen Partner uns erleben, um uns selbst
im Spiegel der anderen zu sehen.
Sylvia Schroll-Machl berichtet auf dem Hintergrund langjäh-
riger Praxis als interkulturelle Trainerin und Wissenschaft-
lerin über viele typische Erfahrungen mit uns Deutschen und
typische Eindrücke von uns.
Es geht ihr aber auch darum, diese Erlebnisse und Erfahrungen aus deutscher Sicht zu beleuchten, damit die nicht-deutschen Partner entdecken, wie wir eigentlich das meinen, was
wir sagen und tun. Zudem beschäftigt sich die Autorin auch
mit den kulturhistorischen Hintergründen, die uns Deutsche
prägen.

Interkulturelle Kommunikation

V&R

Alexander Thomas /
Eva-Ulrike Kinast /
Sylvia Schroll-Machl (Eds.)
**Handbook of Intercultural
Communication and Cooperation**
Basics and Areas of Application

Translated by Charlotte Weston-Horsmann.
2nd revised edition 2010. 412 pages with 23
figures and 14 tables, paperback
ISBN 978-3-525-40327-3

Intercultural competence and collaboration with individuals from diverse
national origins are today important skills. This handbook comprehends an
overall strategic concept for interculturality in corporations.

The ability to communicate with people from diverse cultural backgrounds
is becoming increasingly important. Many employers consider intercultural
competence to be a key criterion for selecting qualified candidates. The
authors discuss practical approaches for intercultural trainings, methodol-
ogy, and evaluation procedures based on current research. They explore the
intercultural factor within corporations particularly as it relates to human
resource development, negotiating, dealing with conflict, and project management. Thoughts on developing an overall strategy for interculturality
round off this handbook.

Alexander Thomas / Eva-Ulrike
Kinast / Sylvia Schroll-Machl (Hg.)
**Handbuch Interkulturelle
Kommunikation und
Kooperation**
Band 1: Grundlagen und Praxisfelder
2., überarb. Auflage 2005. 463 Seiten
mit 23 Abb. und 14 Tab., kartoniert
ISBN 978-3-525-46172-3

Alexander Thomas / Stefan Kammhu-
ber / Sylvia Schroll-Machl (Hg.)
**Handbuch Interkulturelle
Kommunikation und
Kooperation**
Band 2: Länder, Kulturen und
interkulturelle Berufstätigkeit
2., durchgesehene Auflage 2007. 398
Seiten mit 7 Abb. und 6 Tab., kartoniert
ISBN 978-3-525-46166-2

Vandenhoeck & Ruprecht

Handlungskompetenz im Ausland
Trainingsprogramme für Manager, Fach- und Führungskräfte

V&R

Emily J. Slate /
Sylvia Schroll-Machl
Beruflich in den USA
Trainingsprogramm für Manager, Fach-
und Führungskräfte
2. Auflage 2009. 173 Seiten, kartoniert
ISBN 978-3-525-49062-4

Katrin Mitterer /
Rosemarie Mimler /
Alexander Thomas
Beruflich in Indien
Trainingsprogramm für Manager, Fach-
und Führungskräfte
2006. 162 Seiten, kartoniert
ISBN 978-3-525-49068-6

Alexander Thomas / Eberhard
Schenk / Wolfgang Heisel
Beruflich in China
Trainingsprogramm für Manager, Fach-
und Führungskräfte
3., überarb. und erw. Auflage 2008.
156 Seiten, kartoniert
ISBN 978-3-525-49050-1

Stefan Schmid / Alexander Thomas
Beruflich in Großbritannien
Trainingsprogramm für Manager, Fach-
und Führungskräfte
2003. 169 Seiten, kartoniert
ISBN 978-3-525-49051-8

Tatjana Yoosefi /
Alexander Thomas
Beruflich in Russland
Trainingsprogramm für Manager, Fach-
und Führungskräfte
2. Auflage 2008. 132 Seiten, kartoniert
ISBN 978-3-525-49056-3

Andreas Brüch /
Alexander Thomas
Beruflich in Südkorea
Trainingsprogramm für Manager, Fach-
und Führungskräfte
3. Auflage 2007. 163 Seiten, kartoniert
ISBN 978-3-525-49058-7

Sylvia Schroll-Machl / Ivan Nový
Beruflich in Tschechien
Trainingsprogramm für Manager, Fach-
und Führungskräfte
2. Aufl. 2009. 144 Seiten, kartoniert
ISBN 978-3-525-49055-6

Alle Bände mit Cartoons von
Jörg Plannerer.

Vandenhoeck & Ruprecht

Vandenhoeck & Ruprecht

This book sheds light on the two sides of German business partnerships in intercultural settings. On the one hand it deals with people working with Germans from their home country as well as with expatriates who have come to live and work in Germany. On the other hand it portrays Germans who have business relations all over the world negotiating with people in business meetings or via telecommunications.

For people from abroad working in Germany it is vital to find out what the German mentality is like in order to orientate themselves and assess situations better. For Germans it is helpful to understand how their non-German partners perceive them. This again will allow them to see themselves as they are seen by others.

The author

Sylvia Schroll-Machl, PhD, is a psychologist who works as a freelance trainer and coach for various companies, organisations and ministries. She offers courses in intercultural training and human resource development. She is currently teaching at several universities and is a member of the Society for Intercultural Education, Training and Research (SIETAR) and the Sociological Study Group for International Problems (SSIP).
URL: www.schroll-machl.de

ISBN 978-3-525-46167-9

9 783525 461679

www.v-r.de